Si

A Woma

Christianity Was Never About God

By: Katilyn Pulcher

CONTENTS

INTRODUCTION

In any system of life, the status quo seeks to maintain itself until violently forced to change. We see this in economies and social groups.... even earthquakes. The very earth we stand on does not budge without a fuss. No matter how great the need for a new status quo, nor how grotesque or oppressive the current one is, its upheaval requires tremendous effort and mass buy-in. Even the upset of the slavery status quo in the United States required a bloody civil war. Although challenging a status quo is a scary endeavor with potentially severe ramifications, it always starts with something as simple as a probing question. The status quo this book questions is religion, and, more specifically, Christianity.

Having suffered religious abuse and patriarchal wounds, plenty of people have questioned and abandoned their former religious beliefs over the years, but they still found themselves clamoring for faith in some kind of higher power. Humans have been letting each other down for years— decades, even centuries— and, in order to cope, have come to believe god is beyond us and only god will help us because no human consistently has. Unable to cultivate faith in others but faced with their inevitable mortality, many people return to their church/mosque/temple attempting to restore their faith in a god. However, a return to church, Christianity, and/or faith in any type of god will not heal patriarchal and religious wounds; only a return to faith in yourself can do that.

For years, as defenseless children, you may have soaked up lies your parents, caretakers, and/or religious leaders proclaimed to be undeniable truths. I did. However, none of us is under any obligation to continue believing what they told us to believe. We each have a chance to reject the status quo and replace it with a status quon't, which would be an ever-evolving state of critical thought and personalized belief systems. As a female, former Baptist turned atheistic feminist, I'll be discussing the ways in which the status quo of Christian communities and patriarchal societies violates basic human rights to safety, love, personal choice, and self-respect, among others. In turn, I encourage each of my readers to challenge the status quos of the communities to which they belong, even if it means exiting those communities or fully renouncing their beliefs, as I did the Christian church. Note that in identifying as a feminist, I simply mean I believe men and women, including those identifying as trans- and cisgendered, are equal and should be treated as such. In identifying as agnostic, I'm admitting that I do not believe in the Christian god, nor any other god as is understood by an organized religion.

Rather than advocate the abandonment of your beliefs and the adoption of my own, I encourage you to think for yourself. As I see it, and I hope you'll see in the pages to come, religion was never about belief, nor was it about god. You don't have to find a church or temple or believe in a new god to find peace; you simply need to find your true self. The status quo is a stagnant state of widespread groupthink in a common belief system and conformity; a status quon't is a dynamic state of widespread free thought and authenticity. I hope we, as a human race, can someday achieve the latter.

1 - THAT'S JUST HOW IT IS... UNTIL IT ISN'T ANYMORE

Centuries ago, people began to ask questions with unknowable answers, such as "what happens when we die?", "why are women different than men?", and "why is his skin darker than mine?". Other people attempted to answer such questions, and the belief in the answers became widespread enough to be considered the status quo, or the existing state of affairs. The believers then formed groups that we now call "religions," "sexists," "racists," and so on. Although these groups were formed based on beliefs in certain answers to these questions, none of those answers could be proven undeniably true.

As the years progressed, asking whether the unknowable answers provided to probing questions *were* true when they didn't *seem* true became the status quon't, or a rejection of the existing state of affairs. The status quon't could lead to public stoning, burning at the stake, or being cast out as a social pariah. Those who rejected the status quo, non-believers, had to choose between community and truth because the community did not believe the truth. Given the options for community were more limited in the early days—determined entirely by geography—many non-believers accepted the status quo and its traditions simply to join the community and gain strength in numbers. The motivation for many of them likely had nothing to do with the beliefs and everything to do with survival. When faced with a choice between trying to survive on your own in the wilderness and being part of a community that hunts, gathers, and cooks together, most people will understandably choose the latter.

Groups based on shared beliefs were meant to bring people together, but often invoked the opposite effect. The "us vs. them," "saved vs. not," "our god vs. your Allah," "black vs. white," etc., mentalities began to push people away rather than bring them in. People began to dehumanize others who held beliefs different than their own. The status quo was one of division in that the price of admission to one group was rejection of all others. The membership dues to stay in each group were beliefs in common stories, regardless of whether those stories were inarguably true. In the year 2017, people need not pay such steep prices of admission and membership dues to find community.

In the 21st century, we are more connected than ever via phones seemingly permanently attached to our hands. We can use these phones to seek out truth without fear of losing community. Other people who share our belief in the truth, rather than in widely-accepted lies, are a call, click, email, or text away. We no longer have to accept the beliefs, traditions, and status quo of our geographical community simply for strength in numbers, especially if it violates our human rights. Given the current state of affairs and the amount of control that is in the hands of special interest groups full of dangerous people masquerading as well-meaning religious folk, it's now imperative that our society seek truth rather than blindly accepting the lies these groups perpetuate.

A lie does not become true simply because more and more people believe it or because the belief persists for a certain length of time. Since the beginning of time, humans have been operating on beliefs (dare I say "lies") they hope and/or fear to be true. Many of these beliefs are in other worldly, omnipotent, all-powerful, authority figures, also called gods. Religions the world over have affected behavior designed to gain approval (hope) or avoid judgment (consequences) from gods who cannot be seen. Fear of these supernatural threats proved more powerful in an exercise of control than fear of physical harm from a human. This is because a human can be physically avoided by moving away from them or altogether extinguished by murdering them; this was not the case for a god. Recognizing fear as the number one source of human motivation and the fear of god as more paralyzing than fear of themselves, religious leaders claimed to have intimate knowledge of gods' wishes in order to influence their followers. Believing they cannot escape god and must do as he says, humans have acted on these alleged divine messages they believe their religious leaders received. Countless hate crimes and wars have been carried out by people who believe a god desired them.

Belief in a god or gods typically goes hand in hand with belief in an afterlife, thus implanting or removing a fear of death, depending on the religion and the believer himself. Some crimes have been carried out by people who believed their divine wanted them to commit them and that they would meet said divine in an afterlife more comforting than this Earth had been to them. Devout Christians, who believe afterlives are spent in either heaven or hell, would likely have been afraid to commit such crimes. Christians believe mass murder is punishable by banishment to hell, and they believe hell is a fiery inferno of eternal suffering. As we can see, religious leaders can influence their followers to do or avoid any number of things—even kill—simply by claiming the directive came from a god.

Religious beliefs aside, we can all agree that we are accountable, first, to each other. If a man is shot in the heart by his fellow man and left alone, he will die. Even if we fear a fiery afterlife or hope for a blessed one in the heavenly skies, our immediate, common fear is of our fellow man with a gun or a knife who can send us there. We can all agree there is no afterlife without a loss of initial life. Even the most devout Christian, wrought with depression, pondering suicide, and seemingly sure of his future in said heavenly skies, clings to the life he has here on earth. If death is no one's first choice, even for those convinced they will have a happy afterlife, then what is drawing all of us to this life on Earth? It's the certainty of this life and the uncertainty of the afterlife. Boiled down, it's a fear of the unknown—the inevitable uncertainty that arises from a question with an unknowable answer.

Proclamations of absolute answers that humans have no way of knowing need to be revoked by all groups. We need not agree on one universal religion, form of sexism, or type of racism, but rather, we must revoke the false beliefs of each group and start over. For example, disproving one religion's beliefs about an afterlife would not make the other religions' beliefs true, in the same way that proving an animal is not a dog does not automatically prove it is a cat. The only way to prove whether there is an afterlife is to die. However, even if I make a brief cameo in said afterlife, say, via cardiac arrest, I cannot be sure the rest of you will go to the same place I did when you die. The answer to the question "what happens when we die?" is, therefore, unknowable. Similarly, the answer to the question, "where did we come from?" is unknowable.

One who has no recollection of ever having been an ape cannot claim evolution as infallible truth. A person who claims such a truth has no explanation for the side by side existence of apes and humans— for why some would evolve and others not. Clearly our brains haven't completely evolved because we are still fighting religious wars today, and some humans are running each other over with their cars. Recognizing our current beliefs as potential tools of control that may have been in the hands of influential people, rather than self-evident truths, is the first step towards challenging the problematic status quo.

Today's status quo involves horrific crimes committed in the name of a god. Such crimes prove that the resolution of the endless debate as to whose god is real, if there even is a god, is a moot debate. This debate does not make the world a better place. By seeking an external god of any kind and, consequently, peace and happiness outside of ourselves, we place happiness beyond our control, possibly falling into a victim mentality if we do not find it. If we believe there is no god, we are only accountable to ourselves, which can be equally scary. Personally, I like the idea of an internal god that dwells within each of us, as us. The only person on earth who can, with 100% certainty, never abandon us, is ourselves. So, if we are to maintain happiness, and we only have control over ourselves, where better to seek god than from within? If god is outside ourselves and not here on earth, we cannot reliably maintain happiness on earth because we don't know if we will ever reach god, and even if we do, that god will not abandon us once we find him or her.

Joan Osborne posed a profound question in her song "What if God Was One of Us." I would like to take it a step further and hypothesize "what if god was all of us?" Regardless of the religion, its followers do not seek to harm their god. If those followers believed god was in all of us, perhaps they would not harm themselves or each other because they would then be harming god. Perhaps instead of committing terrible crimes and explaining them away as "part of god's plan," they would think twice before acting, because god's plan would also be their plan. Humans don't want to be blamed for heinous crimes or gross abuse and the motivation behind either, any more than a hypothetical, benevolent, supernatural being does.

Similarly, if one believes god dwells within him, the saving grace from any consequences of his crimes extends no further than his own human reach. It would be more difficult, for most, to commit egregious crimes against humanity with no divine safety net.

Think of what could happen if you believe god is within you. Questions of god would become not "who is he?" but "who am I?" Answers to the latter are knowable in an absolute sense and could provide immense comfort once understood. It can be difficult to feel deserving of something beyond yourself, but you are, at the absolute least, deserving of your own love. If you believe that god's love for you and your love for yourself are one and the same, then it is within your control to find lasting love and peace. Believing that god dwells within you, as you, would also make your life much easier to lead, for you would only need to heed your feelings to know what to do. We all feel pain, fear, joy, loneliness, anger, and other emotions at various times in our lives; this is a fact, regardless of whether we all agree on it. Given we all have the same array of feelings, it seems to make more sense to use them as our guideposts for how to live our lives than to use a god, whom not everyone can agree on, as such a guiding force. It also seems logical to accept that since the same range of feelings dwells within all of us, then "god" dwells within all of us. If god dwells within us, as us, we also need not be exactly alike to be deserving of god's love. We can have different skin tones, be of different genders, sound differently, think differently, and so on.

Think of what could happen if you believe god is within every other person. Recognizing the many forms god takes in all the different people in the world, you would try to help others find their *own* way, not your way. You might reach out to others more, beckoning the god that also dwells within them. Rather than praying by yourself in your room at night, you would call your neighbor and ask them for help. If people agreed that something needed to be done, then it would be up to them to do it. They would not sit back and wait for divine intervention because together they are the divine. How many people have knelt down at night praying to god for things their fellow man could have given them had they been brought up in conversation?

In this information age, we have a unique opportunity to be aware of problems in the world but are often stalled at the point of fixing them, afraid of challenging the status quo. Many of us, when asked for help, have been compelled toward inaction because we know that we cannot make an impact alone. Others have not lifted a finger due to their very belief in god—that he will help, and humans need not try. Others have not offered helping hands because they believe their god doesn't want them to.

The wealth of information available to all people is the very weapon that equips us to change the status quo. We can overturn the pattern of waiting for divine intervention upheld by generations before us, not because we know *better*, but because we know *more*. We have access to the thoughts of people who think differently and hold different beliefs than we do, and we can rally resources from around the world in a matter of minutes. All that's missing is a unified belief in the value of all types of humankind and the lives they're currently living. Believing god dwells within humankind and, therefore, that in order for god to help means we will need to help, will move us forward.

RELIGIOUS MIS-TEACHINGS

2 – THE MONSTER IN THE SKY

When you were a kid, were you ever afraid there was a monster in your closet, or perhaps under your bed? If you were like me, you had your mom or dad check the closet and under the bed for monsters before they tucked you in, so you'd know it was safe to sleep. After my mom turned on that light in the closet and checked under the bed with a flashlight, only to find old shoeboxes and toys, I knew I was safe and drifted off to sleep. However, the one monster she could never fully convince me I was safe from was god. My parents told me I couldn't see god but that he could always see me, so even turning on the light in the closet couldn't convince me he wasn't coming to get me. They had also taught me that god had more power than they and could send me to a fiery place called hell forever. They effectively instilled in me a fear of an invisible monster from whom they couldn't protect me. This was my first recollection of unshakeable anxiety and vulnerability.

I was raised Baptist, turned Methodist, and wound up agnostic. From a very young age, my parents and Baptist grandparents taught me that I was inherently bad and needed to be forgiven for my sins and saved by Jesus Christ. Unless I was saved, I would be cast into hell when I died. If I was saved, I would live in heaven with god forever. I fully believed these teachings, not because I'm stupid, but because childhood is a period of time marked by the complete absence of doubt. If one can convince a child that Santa Claus travels the world jumping down chimneys all night, one can surely convince a child that a magical father figure lives in the sky who controls their fate for all eternity. And so, it was done. I was spoon-fed this "truth" and wholeheartedly believed it. All parents confess to their children at some point that Santa Claus isn't real, as did mine. But, I was on my own to figure out that the Christian God isn't real.

I knew I couldn't go to hell until after I died, so I became extremely afraid of death. I learned that sickness could lead to death, and for a few weeks when I was two years old, I walked around with my hands in the air afraid of dirt and germs. In fifth grade, I learned about the AIDS virus and became deathly afraid of public toilet seats, to the point of peeing my pants at school. Then came the obsessive-compulsive handwashing, to the point that my hands became raw and red, cracked and bleeding. All of these were symptoms of one common fear—germs lead to sickness, sickness leads to death, death leads to hell, and no one on earth can help me prevent that from happening.

At five years old, my alleged saving grace came when I was told that Jesus could prevent my going to hell. I was told to recite a prayer asking Jesus for forgiveness and to save me from myself. Three key losses occurred when I had to do this. Loss #1 was of innocence. Five-year-old children who are not imminently being confronted with death are not supposed to be thinking about it for they have only recently been given life. Now acutely aware of death, I had lost my right to a carefree existence in childhood. Loss #2 was of a sense of safety. I was being held accountable to someone I could not see or hear, and my safety from a horrible fate was now entirely beyond my control. I also would not find out if my prayer to be saved had worked until I died, and I was scared it wouldn't be enough. Loss #3 was of good feelings about myself. I had been forced to admit that no matter what I do or think, I am inherently bad, and someone who is better needs to save me because of that fact. At five years old, still brand new to this world, I was already afraid of how and when I would leave it.

Baptists, or at least those who raised me, do not believe in confessing their sins to a priest because they believe only god can forgive sins. Personally, I would have preferred to confess mine to a priest because I would have heard an audible "you're forgiven." I never heard that from god, so I was never quite sure he forgave me. Prayer also never made me feel loved by god. To me, love means feeling heard, understood, and valued. Having confessional conversations by myself (prayers) with someone who could not verbally answer me certainly never made me feel heard. Having to confess to that someone that I'm sinful, bad, and sorry for who I am made me feel worthless instead of valued. The whole experience of prayer and confession made me feel awful and anxious.

I had learned in church that in order to actually be forgiven, I needed to truly be sorry for my sins, in addition to asking god for his forgiveness. Having been taught that god was all-knowing, I knew he'd know if I was just saying I was sorry but didn't actually feel remorse. I then concluded that I'd never be truly forgiven because deep down I didn't feel sorry for a lot of the sins I confessed. To confess or not to confess was not a question of my guilt feelings, but, rather, of the classification of my actions as sins by the Bible or church. Other times, I was truly sorry for what I'd done or said, but then I would repeat the same sin. This left me confused about whether even I knew for sure that I was sorry given that I kept doing the same "bad" thing over and over. It was a never-ending spiral of anxiety, fueled by the knowledge that I could not stop sinning, nor could I control whether god forgave me or not. As I saw it, going to heaven or hell was a coin toss. I went on like this until I finally gave up prayer and my religion nearly twenty years later.

Allow me to provide some examples of the sins I was taught to confess. I wasn't truly sorry for some, dare I even say most, because they felt natural to me. When I was sexually attracted to boys during puberty (considered the sin of lust, in the Christian church), I wasn't sorry, but I confessed that I was. When I wanted to try alcohol at the age of sixteen to see how it made me feel (considered the sin of drunkenness), I wasn't sorry, but I confessed that I was. When I refused to submit to a man in a romantic relationship, I wasn't sorry though *First Timothy 2:11-12* told me I should be. *First Timothy 2:11-12* reads: *"Let a woman learn quietly with all submissiveness. I do not permit a woman to teach or to assume authority over a man; rather, she is to remain quiet."* Thinking for myself instead of deferring to a man was considered a sin by those in my Baptist church, even mentioned in the Bible they preached. I wasn't willing to actually stop thinking for myself, but I did want to please my parents, who followed the rules in the Bible. So, I thought for myself and lied to god about being sorry for having done so.

As I understood it, forgiveness following my confessions would mean I was in good standing with god, and being "saved" would mean I was going to heaven when I died. After I was "saved" at the age of five, meaning I prayed the magic words, I developed anxiety about whether I could be "unsaved" at a future point in time. Among my fears was a fear that I could sin and then die before I was able to confess and request forgiveness. As mentioned above, I was afraid god knew I wasn't sorry for the "sins" I was confessing, would revoke his decision to save me, and then would send me to hell anyway. Sometimes I was afraid my salvation only lasted until the next "horrible" sin I committed. Other times I was afraid my magic prayer wasn't enough, and I would need to be baptized to truly get to heaven. The list of my fears went on and on.

No one could dispel my salvation-related fears because they all gave different answers to my question: "How do I know if I'm saved and will go to heaven when I die?" It's much easier to believe the answer to a question if you get the same one from everyone you ask. If you type "2+2" into every calculator you can find and they all say the answer is "4," it's easy to believe the sum is 4. Such was not the case with this particular question. My parents and grandparents taught me the differing views of the different religions. "Catholics believe you have to work your way to heaven." "Methodists believe you only need to ask Jesus once, through prayer, to save you and that you can't ever lose your salvation." "Baptists believe you need to be baptized in holy water in order to go to heaven." As I heard each differing view, it became clear to me that nobody actually knew the answer to my question and that going to heaven or hell was beyond our control. For example, I could choose to skip being baptized and pray the salvation prayer, but then find out when I died that the Baptists were right about getting into heaven. It would be too late for me.

I was never sure what my parents believed about how to get to heaven, why all these other people believed different things, and why each was so confident they were right. I also never understood why, if my parents loved me, they didn't have me baptized as a child and sent to a confession booth in a Catholic church, just to be safe. Regardless of salvation, whether it occurred, how it occurred, and how long it lasted, I knew one thing for certain: I would only find out if I had been saved when I died. From the time I realized this until the time I became agnostic, I was terrified of death. My parents, grandparents, and church had successfully put "the fear of god" in me.

From my perspective, god was even more terrifying than a monster in the closet would have been. A monster in the closet could be locked in there. It could only get me if I let it out of the closet. It could only hurt me physically, and at that, it could only do so in my human lifetime. God, however, could not be contained in a closet, can see and hear whatever I'm doing at all times, could physically or emotionally harm me, and could hurt me not only in this human lifetime, but potentially forever. Many of us have read *1984*, or at least seen the television show "Big Brother" and noticed the inevitable mental and emotional meltdown from the anxiety that a complete lack of privacy causes the participants. Such is the life of a child in a religiously fanatic home, feeling she is under the constant gaze of god. This is one of the many ways in which religion can be used as a weapon. When it is used as a weapon, it is considered abuse. The obsessive handwashing and compulsive praying, in my case, were the post-traumatic stress disorder symptoms of the religious abuse I suffered.

3 – THE 800,000-WORD RULE BOOK

All ethical codes can be derived from one simple principal: Love your neighbor as yourself, or worded differently, treat your neighbor as you wish to be treated. However, this rule will ONLY serve as a guide if you do, in fact, love and treat yourself well. In order to love ourselves, we have to truly know ourselves. Unfortunately, the Christian churches I grew up in did not teach self-discovery and self-love, nor did the Bible verses they preached. They preached that humans are inherently sinful and not deserving of even their own love, but that god will love them anyway. Their primary goal was to help their members know a "god" outside themselves (who allegedly lives in heaven) and feel "his" love for them, rather than to cultivate a love for themselves. This goal conflicts with the common knowledge that one cannot have a healthy, successful relationship with another—even god —if she does not love herself. In fact, if another person loves me but I do not love myself enough to believe I am worthy of their love, I will mistrust it, be unable to feel it, and, thus, find no comfort in it. Therefore, it follows that the first step toward a moral existence is to love yourself.

Proverbs 16:18 reads: *Pride goes before destruction, and a haughty spirit before a fall.* This verse was usually cited to me by my parents or grandparents when I was proud of an accomplishment—be it a report card full of A+'s or a home run at my softball game. This constant verbal reminder led to my personality trait of "waiting for the other shoe to drop." Unfortunately, I interpreted the "lesson" as "the only way to avoid a crisis is to never be proud of myself (i.e., never get too comfortable)." The double whammy to my self-esteem was that being proud of and loving myself was a bad idea for two reasons: 1) it would cause subsequent crises in my life, and 2) it was completely undeserved due to my sinner status.

The entire 14th chapter of the book of Luke in the Bible goes beyond discouraging self-love to even encouraging hatred of your neighbors. In this chapter, Jesus invited a bunch of people over for dinner and got all pissed off that everyone had excuses for why they couldn't

21

make it, such as their family engagements. Verse 26 is especially scathing and reads: *"If anyone comes to me and does not hate his own father and mother, wife and children, brothers and sisters—yes, and even his own life—he cannot be my disciple."* The Cliff's notes version—hate yourself and everyone except for me, and follow me. Imagine if a random bearded guy walked into a Walgreen's proclaiming this… do you think people would follow him? I sure as hell wouldn't. I don't want someone else's love if the price is self-hatred. I've personally had a pit in my stomach on several occasions from someone telling me to hide my talents so he or she feels more secure—so I don't "feel too proud" and leave him or her thinking I deserve better. I don't associate that pit in my stomach with the feeling of being loved by another. Hate should never be a requirement for love: it's an oxymoron to think otherwise.

The book of Romans also discourages self-love. *Romans 3:23* reads: *For all have sinned and fall short of the glory of God.* The underlying message, through my interpretation, was: You are not good enough to even deserve god's love. Unfortunately, devout believers (such as my former self) absorb these verses as absolute truth, thereby willingly disabling their ability to love themselves. Given they cannot love themselves and use that as their guide for how to treat other human beings, they turn to the

Bible for guidance. The approximately 800,000 words describe "lessons" and rules that can be interpreted any number of ways and used to instruct human beings on how to treat each other. Let's start with the ten commandments (paraphrased from *Deuteronomy 5: 6-21*):

1. You shall have no other gods before me.

2. You shall not make idols and bow down to or serve them.

3. You shall not take the name of the LORD your god in vain.

4. Remember the Sabbath day, to keep it holy... you shall not do any work... on it

5. Honor your father and your mother.

6. You shall not murder.

7. You shall not commit adultery.

8. You shall not steal.

9. You shall not bear false witness against your neighbor.

10. You shall not covet...anything that is your neighbor's.

Piece of cake, right? The original top Ten listicle. It's the 21st century, and we like efficiency—we like lists.

Never lie, want anything someone else has, forget it's Sunday, or say "oh my god!" and god will approve! Good luck having any friends if you have to tell them that yes, they do look really worn out this morning (and fat in

23

those pants)! Forget connecting with anyone on Facebook—you might want what someone else has! Be sure to pull up your browser and sleep through an online sermon this Sunday because even if your heart's not in it, you've been commanded to "show up." After all, god takes attendance.

The Christian way of life, as preached by the churches I grew up in and paraphrased through me, is to do your best to keep all the commandments and when you inevitably fail, ask god to forgive you. If you're Catholic, rather than asking god to forgive you, you ask the priest to forgive you in what they call a "confession." When Catholics confess their sins, in order to atone, they are often instructed to say a Hail Mary prayer or other type of prayer a certain number of times, depending on what the priest deems to be merited based on the severity of their sins. Such was the birthplace of the phrase "throwing up a Hail Mary," though it is often used in reference to a long touchdown pass in American football. Regardless of context, the meaning behind the phrase, as I understand it, is that if you can't help yourself, throw up a few Hail Mary prayers as a last resort and hope for forgiveness. In other words, beg for forgiveness, rather than ask for permission.

According to the New Testament, God himself knew humans were incapable of keeping his ten commandments, so he sent his son to earth to sort it out.

The church I grew up in then taught us that rather than doing confessions like the Catholics, all we needed to do was believe Jesus died for our sins and ask him (through prayer) to save us. This is the magic prayer I recited at five years old and referred to in chapter two.

Personally, I had a hard time believing that saying a magic prayer to Jesus one time would take care of everything, so I tried to keep the ten commandments—just in case. As the years went on, I realized I couldn't consistently follow all the rules because many of them defy my natural instincts. I was exhausted from trying and weary of feeling ashamed of my natural self. So, I saw myself as having two options. Option 1 was to commit the "sins" without even trying not to then ask for forgiveness (the Hail Mary). After all, my church leaders told me that God has to love and forgive me whether I try not to do them or I consciously choose to—that's God's grace! Option 2 was to lose my religion and remove my guilt for things I didn't think were all that bad. I tried Option 1 for over twenty years and suffered enormously in the process, and I arrived simultaneously at my wit's end and Option 2 a few years later—but we'll get to that in another chapter.

The problem with living your life according to a set of rules, and in particular, the ten commandments, is that it leads to unhealthy absolute thinking. Look at them again—there is no mention of moderation in the ten commandments. There are no footnotes. There is no fine print. Everything has been expressed as unconditional. Right or wrong. Black or white. Heads or tails. Isn't it ironic that the ridges on an American quarter are on the outside edges, between heads and tails, for the precise purpose of "getting a grip"? The followers of these ten rules have introduced a host of problems into this world because they have tried to compartmentalize people into two groups: Heads — "all good" because they follow the commandments, and Tails — "all bad" because they don't. All humans are a mix of both good and bad by nature, so attempting to stay in the "all good" category and failing repeatedly leads to unhealthy shame. Likewise, being categorized as "all bad" and given no credit for your good qualities leads to unhealthy shame. The answer to lasting peace has been in our piggybanks, pockets, and coin purses for years; the only place to get a grip is the third side of the coin, between the two extremes—the rough-edged, proverbial shade of gray.

It's not only impossible to follow the ten commandments in totality to be considered "all good," but it can also be impossible to follow some of them individually. In fact, to follow them absolutely, meaning 100% of the time, would be unwise and even unsafe for many of us. Early Christians originally attempted to follow them because the Old Testament discusses god's plan to grant his mercy only to those who follow his commandments. However, *John 3:16* from the New Testament changed everything. The verse reads: *"For god so loved the world that he gave his only begotten son, that whosoever believeth in him shall not perish but have everlasting life."* How unfair! Right? Whoever lived before Jesus came to earth had to follow a set of impossible rules in an attempt to get into heaven, and everyone alive afterwards just had to believe that a bearded hipster named Jesus was the son of God and they were saved. Regardless of the raw deal handed to those alive B.C., if the god that Christians believe in has shown that even *he* is on board with changing the rules when they need to evolve, then why are Christians still holding on to rules from thousands of years ago?

Let's examine each of the commandments:

1. *You shall have no other gods before me.* Every Muslim, Jew, Buddhist, or other religious but non-Christian person is in violation of this commandment. It's not possible for everyone to follow this commandment because plenty of people are raised in non-Christian homes and parts of the world. Christians believe that other religions of the world, who follow their own gods, are in

direct violation of the "real" laws (commandments) and need to be saved and taught the "right" way of life. There is no harmonious state of agreeing to disagree under this commandment. Being forced to follow others' commands instead of choosing to do that very thing of your own free will can also lead to violent rebellions. Examples include the Christian Crusades and the American attempt to force democracy on the Middle East in the 2000s. On a lesser scale, any parent who has attempted to force a toddler to go to bed instead of letting him tire himself out can attest to such a kicking and screaming rebellion. Forcing this commandment on everyone would not lead to a more peaceful world, so following it in an absolute sense is unwise and unsafe.

2. *You shall not make idols and bow down to or serve them.* This commandment does not define the word "idol," so it's impossible to be sure you're correctly following it, if you even try. Does it mean you shouldn't make a statue and bow to it, or is it less literal in that you shouldn't be a fangirl of someone and "make" them an idol in your mind and heart? For instance, did everyone who

watched the show American Idol break the commandment? Is everyone who considers themselves part of the Beyhive breaking this commandment? The Baptist church I attended as a kid took this lesson to an extreme. Trolls were a popular toy when I was a child. They were tiny, naked creatures with jewels for belly buttons and crazy colored hair. The marketing campaign suggested children treat them like genies and make wishes while touching the jewels on their bellies in order for the wishes to come true. My church caught wind of this and dedicated an entire sermon to condemning that behavior because they considered it idolizing something other than the lord, as well as praying to the troll instead of God. Of course, this was deemed a sin that needed to be confessed and forgiven. See how crazy that is? These people actually believed a child was sinning if she wished for mac 'n' cheese for dinner on her toy troll's belly.

3. *You shall not take the name of the LORD your god in vain.* This one is impossible for children, specifically, to follow because they learn to speak by mimicking the words of those around them. If children watch TV and hear the phrase "oh my

god!" then they are bound to say it at some point. If they hear it enough and say it enough, it will become a habit that is hard to kick. The motivation to stop will also be low because "everyone else is doing it." I would argue that attempting to follow this commandment is both impossible and a waste of time.

4. *Remember the Sabbath day, to keep it holy...you shall not do any work...on it.* Ah yes, the commandment to do no work on Sundays. Somehow, most Christians aren't out there trying to shut down hospitals and fire departments on Sundays, yet the commandment does not begin with a logical caveat, such as "except for doctors, nurses, and firefighters." Millions would die every year if hospitals had to be closed on Sundays. Following this commandment 100% of the time is simply unsafe. It was also written before hospitals existed, but we'll get to the application of rules that pre-dated certain conditions in a later chapter.

5. *Honor your father and your mother.* This commandment completely excuses cases of child abuse and ignorantly assumes all parents love their

children. In the case of abuse, honoring a parent violates the child's right to self-respect. Modern society does not ask a rape victim to honor her perpetrator, so to ask, for example, a victim of fatherly incest to honor her father is appalling. What's interesting to me is that god violated his own son's right to self-respect by demanding that he honor and love him. Parents who love their children do not willingly put them in situations where they would be killed by an angry mob. And yet, god allegedly did this very thing with his own son—sending Jesus to earth knowing he would eventually be nailed to a cross and left to die. Could this have been the birthplace of "do as I say, not as I do"?

Christian parents have also been taught the concept of original sin, and many use that to explain away their terrible parenting. These parents are taught by certain Christian churches (and the ones I attended, in particular—lucky me!) to believe that all people, even newborn children, are sinful (bad). This commandment backs up their belief that they can do no wrong and need to be honored at all costs. No matter how they treat the child, if she acts out in an extremely unsavory way, they feel justified in saying, "We didn't teach her to be that way; she just came into this world like that. It was her original sin."

6. *You shall not murder.* This one is a no brainer for most humans and very easy to follow 100% of the time. However, the fact that someone felt it needed to be said in order to be upheld is disheartening. It would not have needed to be said if Christians were fully allowed to love themselves and value their own lives. All living things have survival instincts. In order to kill another or oneself, a denial of this instinct and the value of a life must exist. Unfortunately, the Christian faith, along with many other religions, can plant such denial. The commandments, in totality, lead to no compassion for one's self and suffering. We learn that we have no value unless we follow them. By failing to follow them, over and over, we also learn that we are never going to be good enough to get to heaven.

The Bible teaches that we're not currently with God when we're alive, but that we will be when we die and go to heaven. This can lessen the motivation to be alive and cause denial of one's own survival instincts. The interpretations of this particular commandment are many, and a number of humans believe there are "righteous" instances in which to commit murder. One could even argue that God himself was an accomplice in the "righteous" murder of his own son (Jesus). He may not have hung him on the cross, but he did put him in the situation that led to his death (*John 3:16* describes God sending Jesus to Earth). A court of law would likely convict God as an accomplice to murder, just as they would a person who drives a getaway car in a homicide case. God even confessed his motive in *John 3:16 ("gave his only begotten son"* to pay for humans' sins). It is no wonder Christians have a hard time interpreting rules and deciding when to follow them when their leader, himself, doesn't follow them 100% of the time. Such a "do as I say, not as I do" dynamic is rampant across the world. Children of addicts are expected to follow rules their parents don't enforce on themselves, and "love" and attention is withheld if the children don't comply. The self-worth of these children is lowered in such an environment because the message is received as "I am unworthy of my leader's unconditional love, but he (or she) is worthy of mine."

7. *You shall not commit adultery.* This commandment assumes all marriages are fulfilling and will continue to be so until death. It can be tough to follow, given marriages are longer these days, and/or unwise to follow if the spouse is abusive. The reason marriages are longer (or at least, supposed to be, given the vows of eternal commitment exchanged) is that people are living longer. It was easier to avoid cheating on a spouse for a lifetime when people only lived thirty-ish years and had access to others they could reach by foot. Now we have tempting pictures on our phones in the palm of our hands, and we can reach almost anyone in the world in 24 hours via airplane.

This commandment is also a difficult one to follow because it can condone martyrdom and suffering. Many well-meaning Christians have entered marriages that became sexless or emotionally vacant, and yet stayed together due to this commandment. Such a situation leads to unhappiness, not only for the married couple, but perhaps even more so, for their children. Often, these children know their parents are staying together "for them," but also that they are unhappy. Thus, they blame themselves for their parents' unhappiness. Other parents overstep their children's boundaries, using them to meet needs their spouse should be fulfilling but isn't. All of these parents model unhealthy relationships for their children. One more ridiculous verse bears repeating here, and that's *Matthew 5:28-29: "But I say to you that everyone who looks at a woman with lustful intent has already committed adultery with her in his heart. If your right eye causes you to sin, tear it out and throw it away. For it is better that you lose one of your members than that your whole body go into hell."* First of all, how would you even know which eye you looked out of? I don't see different things out of my eyes; it's one combined image, so if I see a sexy man and want to kiss him, I would have to gouge both of my eyes out and become blind. EVERY- LAST- PERSON on the planet would be blind if this rule were followed because we can't control our lust, nor can we avoid seeing all attractive people besides our spouses or partners.

8. *You shall not steal.* I can get on board with this one. Pay for things or ask to borrow them, plain and simple. But let's think back to why this one would even need to be said. Money didn't always

exist. Rights of ownership used to be murky, and people used to have to figure out how to share. If you took something from someone's house, how could they really prove they owned it in the first place? This commandment would have been hard to follow in the old days. It's still hard to follow for many people who are born into poverty or have come upon such hardship that they cannot survive without stealing things they can't afford to buy. If humans loved themselves and, thus, were able to love and give to others, we would want to share, and others would not have to steal. It's hard not to steal when the minimum wage is so low in certain states and cities, and, in my view, the wage is low because of a lack of self-love and consequent compassion from those who regulate it.

9. *You shall not bear false witness against your neighbor.* This is the Biblical way of saying, "don't lie." If people followed this rule 100% of the time, the world would run rampant with widespread panic and emotional chaos. It is not possible to have a healthy relationship with another person without a few white lies. For instance, if people weren't allowed to say, "it's going to be okay," meanwhile knowing full well

that it's not, then no relationship would be able to provide comfort to the other person. If the full truth about every data breach or disease outbreak were widely broadcast, the public could panic, and people would be afraid to leave their houses or keep their money in the banks. Currently, such events are often downplayed and said to be "under control." Without these white lies, the world could become an angry, anxious place, so following this commandment 100% of the time is unwise.

10. *You shall not covet...anything that is your neighbor's.* Ha, really? How do we achieve this in 2017 without willfully going blind and deaf? The only way to NEVER want what someone else has is to not know it exists. This was MAYBE achievable in the old days where families lived isolated lives on vastly expansive farmland. Now people literally live on top of each other in cities the world over. Even if we wanted to spread everybody out to avoid "coveting," we couldn't— the world is overpopulated. This is an example of a commandment that is impossible to follow, individually. Also, if we didn't want what others had, a lot of us wouldn't grow professionally and

personally as much as we have, so following this commandment is unwise.

The ten commandments aside, there are plenty of other Bible verses about not getting drunk, eating too much meat, envying things others have, or being a homosexual male. Verses in the books of Corinthians and Galatians make it explicitly clear that if a person does any of these things, he will not get into heaven. And yet, verses in the book of John talk about Jesus turning barrels and barrels of water into wine to show "his glory." That's just rude. It's the same thing as baking trays of brownies and bringing them to your friend's house when you know he is trying to diet and lose weight. Jesus was essentially saying, "Look how great I am. I can make all this wine, but you shouldn't drink it because I will harshly judge you and not let you into heaven if you do." The point is, the Bible is full of too many conflicting messages to be considered absolute truth and full of too many conflicting rules for one to follow them all. Further, if a person tries to follow all of the rules he will become overwhelmed with anxiety and lead a miserable life. Personally, I don't see the point of living a miserable life that you're sure you have (after all, you're here reading this book, aren't you?) in hopes of a better life that you're not sure you'll have (in heaven when you die).

The Bible has a "solution" for not being able to keep track of all the rules, as well. *Matthew 5:48* sums it up for us: *You therefore must be perfect, as your heavenly Father is perfect.* We all know we are flawed, imperfect beings. So, talk about sucking the wind out of our sails. This verse does not pose a S.M.A.R.T. (specific, measurable, attainable, reasonable, time-sensitive) solution—thank you, Corporate America. We're never going to get there. As a lifelong perfectionist, I can speak to the experience of trying to be perfect—it's losing a new game every day. I can always be better or worse in one area or another, but never perfect in all of them, not even one. This goal creates shame, disdain, and depression. I'd advise throwing it out the window, along with the rest of the rules in the Bible. Follow your heart, not a list.

The point of the analysis in this chapter was to get you thinking about the rules according to which you've been living your life, regardless of whether they are the ones written in the Bible. Rules need not be black or white, nor must they stay forever the same. Even god's rules changed when the New Testament was written. Consider the Supreme Court of the United States' decision to make same-sex marriage legal in 2015. While it had been a rule for the longest time that homosexuals couldn't marry, homosexual people did not accept this rule. They still became romantically involved with each other, and they fought to have the rule overturned. These people believed the rule should change, lived their lives as if it were already changed, and then made sure that it was. I dream of a world in which the same tactic is used for other nonsensical rules from the Bible. If advocates for equal rights could influence the text of the Bible as they have our laws in America, we might be closer to national peace and, by proxy, world peace.

4 – FORBIDDEN FRUIT

Anyone who has ever been told they can't have something can attest to how much more enticing that thing can become simply because it's forbidden. In the story of the Garden of Eden, Eve ate an apple that she was not supposed to eat. This was the birthplace of the phrase "forbidden fruit." If Eve was truly a real person, we could posit that maybe she didn't even want an apple that day until god told her she couldn't have one. Things people wouldn't even dream of wanting can suddenly become appealing, simply because they're forbidden. I actually believe this to be one of the top reasons people smoke even one cigarette. Think about it – the easiest thing we do in life is breathe. What reason would anyone have for choosing to do something that makes our most basic function harder, besides to rebel?

Prohibiting certain actions, thoughts, or indulgences, rather than encouraging them in moderation, can severely handicap a person's emotional development. Most of us prefer to decide for ourselves what we want and don't want, as well as in what quantity. When that right is stripped away from us, it can make us resent the person who forbade it. Worse yet, it can make us distrust our instincts by teaching us that our first instinct as to what we want and/or need is wrong and to look for guidance elsewhere. Both our autonomy and emotional security are, consequently, stunted. Both effects came to fruition in my life.

Alcohol, drugs, and sex were all outlawed in my household growing up. My parents were teetotalers during my childhood and adolescence, and nobody breathed a word about sex. My parents never had "the talk" with me, but from what I learned in church, sex was not to be discussed or had until you are married. This extremely strict environment felt like a prison, and I rebelled against the rules as soon as I left home for college. I drank way past my limit for the first few years of college, and once I started having sex, I slept with several men. Having been deprived for so long, I felt the desire to overindulge to "balance out." I'm certainly not the only one to overindulge, either. There's a time-honored tradition in college of taking twenty-one shots on your twenty-first birthday. The drive to do so is huge because you've been waiting so long to have a right to those drinks that you want ALL of them at once. Having come out of both phases of life now—extreme deprivation and overindulgence—I find that I like the middle ground. I was marginally happier drinking a lot and having a lot of sex than I was abstaining from both altogether, but I have found that neither overindulgence nor total abstinence feels natural or makes me happy.

In the absence of alcoholism or sex addiction, in which a person has no control over their urges, I don't think it is healthy to completely abstain from sex or drinking alcohol. Physical benefits of abstaining aside, this can negatively affect one's emotional stability. Emotional health is just as important as physical health, and both extreme deprivation and overindulgence lead to unhappiness. This can be the case with food as well. Most extremely rigid diets are ineffective because the person's emotional health starts to suffer too much from the deprivation of the joy of eating their favorite foods and of social interaction. The dieters must often avoid eating out with friends who don't have the same restrictions in order to avoid temptation.

Abstaining from sex, alcohol, delicious food, or other enjoyable things requires extreme discipline and a large dose of fear. I abstained from sex and alcohol while I lived at home because I was afraid of my family's judgment and punishment. Further, I abstained from sex for a couple years in college because I was still religious and afraid of the wrath of god. Folks who aren't raised in religious households may abstain from drinking for fear of losing control—it's known to lower your inhibitions. Others may abstain from sex from a basic fear of intimacy, or perhaps due to bodily insecurities. The types of fear that lead a person to deprive himself or herself are endless, but there is always at least one present. A life of deprivation for physical health is no healthier than a life of overindulgence because of the effect the ever-present fear will have on one's emotional health. Studies often tout the physical dangers of drinking alcohol (liver cancer, etc.) or having unprotected sex (HPV and HIV, etc.) but not the emotional dangers of abstaining altogether (loneliness, depression, anxiety, etc.). While one need not drink alcohol or have sex if she doesn't want to, she should at least not be afraid of such a choice, no matter what she chooses.

It can also be very painful to have someone forbid you from doing something you know you would never dream of doing. This is another way in which parents and teachers commonly doubt their children's instincts and disrespect them. I always thought I was a good kid and knew I was doing the best I could to make my parents proud, so when my mom screamed in the car one day, "Don't get pregnant!", I was humiliated. I had just begun my first romantic relationship. My first thoughts when she screamed at me were, "Is that what you think of me? That I'm going to be reckless and thwart my bright future with an unplanned pregnancy? I know better than that, but why don't you think I do?" As with most messages in my childhood, this one wasn't deliberately meant to imply ill intent on my part. The message was intended to cover all the bases of possible shenanigans I could get myself into and to ensure I knew which ones were "acceptable."

School teachers attempt to cover their bases by using the phrase "history repeats itself" and teaching students about horrific crimes committed against humanity. In the American school system, we all learn about slavery, the Holocaust, and racism at young, impressionable ages as if children are born into the world with the ideas that we are anything less than equal and that mass genocides should be committed. This is another example of teaching children not to trust their instincts. It shows that many adults believe that unless they tell their children not to enslave, rape, murder, or kill people, they will. I spend a lot of time in New York and have lived in

Chicago for nearly ten years, both very populous cities. I have yet to meet a person that would ever dream of killing an entire race of people, so for the life of me, I cannot understand why we spent so much time learning about the Holocaust in school. Ignorance truly is bliss, but we rob our children of that bliss. Maybe I'm wrong, but from what I've seen, the temptation to kill people, especially on such a massive scale, does not exist in the vast majority of people, so mass genocide really needn't be talked about at such length. Instead of placing endless demands on children to behave perfectly and stressing out their fragile brains trying to remember all the rules, much more trust should simply be placed in their basic instincts.

I believe we should trust that children's instincts are basically good and that they will choose not to harm others. Once a person tries to harm others, a learning opportunity will arise, but even at that, this lesson need not be extreme and filled with scare tactics. It's just as important for parents to teach their children that they can trust their feelings and instincts to guide them as it is to teach them that violence is not the proverbial "answer." For instance, if a little boy pushes his friend down on the playground because that friend took his ball, the mom does not need to sit him down and use the history of the Vietnam War to explain that acts of violence are wrong. In fact, she doesn't even need to tie the current situation to a historical example. She could simply ask her son, "Does it make you feel bad when someone pushes you down? Do you want to make your friend feel that way?" and the child will understand that he should not have pushed his friend. This empathic approach is more likely to stick with the child and guide his future actions because he will have learned both not to be violent and why.

Abstinence only sex education and the D.A.R.E. (Drug Abuse Resistance Education) programs are the perfect examples that proved forbidding things does not always lead to prevention and can, in fact, encourage partaking. The numbers show that abstinence only education is less effective at keeping teens safe. The new approach of teaching students about the various forms of birth control and how to wear condoms has been statistically proven to lower the number of STD infections and pregnancies among teens. This approach assumes teens want to have sex, but also that they want to be safe. The respect for both natural instincts (sex and survival), combined with an empathic teaching approach, is crucial.

I remember being in the D.A.R.E. program in elementary school and learning about all sorts of situations I didn't encounter until my late teenage years, others I didn't encounter until my mid-twenties, and still others I have yet to be presented with (I'm currently in my thirties). Funding for the program was drastically cut when government reports were produced that challenged the efficacy of the program. As a D.A.R.E. graduate, I can vouch that the program taught me about drugs I wouldn't dream of taking and did not even have the option to take. I had no idea where to get crack and heroin when I was in elementary school, and if I did, I wouldn't have wanted to try either—and I still don't. Plenty of people have a fear of needles, and that fear alone would keep them from trying heroin, not the lecture they heard from a police officer in the D.A.R.E. program when they were ten years old. Rather than teaching young children about all the horrible things they can be offered, we need to protect their innocence. We need to raise them in homes where they won't encounter such things. Rather than telling them about the neighbor down the street who hates black people, we need to focus on being accepting of all race in our own families. Kids mimic their parents, not their grown neighbors.

Rather than teaching the kids what to say when someone offers them cocaine, we need to move them to neighborhoods where they won't even be offered cocaine, if we have the means. Other kids in the program romanticized drugs after learning about them in the D.A.R.E. presentations. The knowledge of how drugs can make their bodies feel more relaxed or more excited, and that their parents and the police didn't want them to take them, made them even more enticing.

Teaching young children about drug use and crimes against humanity has one other unwanted, but often neglected, side effect—it sets the bar. Kids who learn about heroin at ten years old might decide smoking weed at age fourteen isn't "all that bad." A teenage boy who has learned about school shootings and then hits his girlfriend may decide, "I'm not so bad—at least I didn't shoot anyone." A young girl who learned about Enron may take a white-collar job later and decide, "I'm not so bad—at least I only embezzle $100 per month." Children learn that extreme violence and intricate financial schemes are bad but may fail to take in the values that these stories should be teaching—don't physically hurt anyone and don't steal anything. I'll reiterate that we need to assume our children don't want to do these things until we see them do them; then we can act on the teachable moment. A child will have no idea what it feels like to kill someone or rob a company but will know what it feels like to fall off her bike or have her favorite toy taken away. Real-time, personal examples are much more effective for teaching moral lessons than ancient, historical examples of war or forbidden fruit.

5 – THE THIRD TESTAMENT

It has baffled me for quite some time how no one ventured to write a Third Testament of the Bible. Somehow, everyone was on board with the New Testament that completely reversed many of the teachings in the Old Testament, but no one wrote a third one to override the ridiculous portions of the New Testament. I don't understand how so many people blindly trust someone (God) who changed the rules. Under the Old Testament, a plethora of rules had to be followed to keep God happy and get into heaven. Under the New Testament, Jesus took all the heat for our crimes, and all we had to do to get in was believe he saved us.

We are quick to become angry with a referee who calls fouls on one team but turns a blind eye to those of the other. Yet, somehow, Christians wholeheartedly trust a god who chooses to take care of people living after his son died but was angry, jealous, and vengeful toward anyone who came before him. It seems dangerous for Christians to assume they are completely safe from the wrath of a god who could easily enlist new disciples to write a third testament that changes the rules yet again.

If a third testament were written, and it condoned homosexuality as a perfectly normal, non-sinful thing, would Christians change their minds about it? Would it dissipate all of the hatred in the world if this testament told us to love everyone, regardless of our differences? In my opinion, no. I think if this hypothetical scenario were to happen, homosexuals would still remember hateful things said to them by people who suddenly change their tune based on the new script. They would sense the insincerity and feel rejected just the same. We cannot successfully teach someone to love by telling them what to love because it could always be insincere. Instead, we must teach them how to love. The dark side of Christianity is not that its followers are taught to love and hate the wrong things or people; it's that they are not taught *how* to love.

Had I the opportunity to write the Third Testament, it would include two key verses. Verse 1 would be the definition of love, which I understand to be a feeling of being heard, understood, safe with, and valued by another. Verse 2 would read: "Love yourself and one another." Personally, I didn't feel loved in church or by my starkly religious parents and grandparents. Strung out from trying to follow the multitude of rules themselves, my mother was perpetually angry and my father perpetually distant. My grandparents couldn't talk about anything without including a Bible verse or trying to evangelize the other participant in the conversation. They simply couldn't deal with their own shame, depression, and anxiety that resulted from religious fanaticism, so they couldn't hear how I truly felt either. I was not understood because I was not heard. And I was not valued for who I am because none of them understood who I was. I only received affection and kind words when I fit the mold cut out for me, and when I didn't, because I forgot, was tired, or was just a being a damn kid, I was punished.

I know I'm not the only person raised in a religious household who felt that way as a kid. It was extremely difficult for me to stop calling the treatment I endured as a child "love" and to break the "honor thy father and mother" commandment. This commandment would be overturned in the Third Testament if I (or anyone, really) wrote it. The commandment wasn't the only reason I held back from realizing the "love" I got from my parents was actually emotional abuse and neglect; societal expectations were another reason. Even those who aren't religious have a hard time questioning the motives behind their parents' actions. We feel the burden of a debt that seemingly cannot be repaid to the people who "gave us life." It's extremely hard to say, "you're not giving me enough or treating me right," to someone who gave you life. We feel guilty wanting more from someone who we wouldn't even exist without. However, anyone who has endured abuse knows there is a difference between life and survival. Our parents give all of us, at a minimum, survival. Religious abuse, however, takes away life. It restricts our choices to a very narrow, permissible scope, limiting our ability to experience many of the joys life has to offer.

Fortunately, by merely understanding the true definition of love, I now know what to offer others and what to look for in the way they treat me. Unfortunately, I didn't come across this particular definition of love until I was twenty-nine years old. Notice the definition in the two verses I drafted for the Third Testament does not describe a way to love, for that way will vary depending on the person receiving the love. In order to truly love someone in a way they can feel, you have to understand them. In order to understand them, you have to hear them and fully absorb what they say makes them feel loved. In order for them to feel safe with you, you must love them in a way they can feel. It all ties together.

Despite the definition of love being simple, sharing it with each other can be extremely difficult. It requires both parties to first journey inward to understand themselves and how they feel love, for we cannot communicate that which we do not know. Surprisingly few of us were allowed to take such a journey inward as kids. The definition of justice—treating similar things similarly and different things differently—should also apply to love but is not allowed to in a dysfunctional family. It is expected that parents treat other people's children differently from their own but not that they treat their own children differently from each other. In a dysfunctional family, Gary Chapman's five languages of love are narrowed to one and applied to all children equally. The children are expected to be grateful for this garden variety love and can be punished in obscene ways for expressing anything other than sheer, even if insincere, elation at having received it.

For example, in my family, the garden varieties of love offered were gifts and words of affirmation—things that could be purchased or said. We were given whatever material things we needed (school supplies, nice clothes, food) and most of the things we wanted (toys, trips to the movies, etc.). Both of my parents grew up rather poor, so from my perspective, they were actually giving my siblings and me the things *they* had wanted as children. What my parents failed to realize is that this strategy would not satisfy their unmet childhood needs because they were now adults. It also would not satisfy the needs of my brother, my sister, and me unless our love language was gifts or words of affirmation.

Physical affection and quality time are two love languages that I felt to be in short supply in my childhood home. Through my own journey inward, I discovered that my language of love is quality time. With an angry mother and workaholic father (a situation I'm sure many of you can relate to), I was starved for quality time and, therefore, love. I often had to avoid spending time with my mother because being around her meant being yelled at and constantly criticized. We shared a house but spent most of our time in different rooms. My dad chose to avoid all of us by working too many hours. He and my mom bought us all the food we could eat, but food isn't love, and I refused to eat it for a time. I was so hungry for kind words and attention that I starved myself in order to get them from society. The comments on my thinness and physical attractiveness rolled in from peers, teachers, and coaches as the pounds began to drop off. I needed the attention and kind words so badly that I couldn't stop striving for them, so I lost more and more weight until my physical health was in danger and I became anorexic. Both my body and soul were starving. I understand that my parents tried their hardest not to deprive us of the material things their parents had withheld, but I believe they misinterpreted what had truly been withheld—love.

Love languages are only useful if deemed important, understood, and communicated. And what better place to communicate them than in the books people are using to guide their lives, such as the Bible. A Third Testament of the Bible would need to serve at least two purposes: 1) to add love, and 2) to remove violence. It has become urgent that these new passages be added to the religious books because our world is growing increasingly hateful and violent.

Any religious group could be a threat in the future if the hatred bred within festers long enough. For example, it is clear that the hatred within the Christian faith has been heightening in recent years because many of their ideals (e.g., no abortion, abstinence-only education, etc.) have been overturned by political institutions. Many of them voted for Donald Trump, a man who has promised to restore Christian-inspired laws such as these in America, and numerous hate crimes have been committed in his name since the 2016 presidential election. A lesson we can learn from the hate crimes and the Christian Crusades is that people can do extremely harmful things if they feel justified, and that some people use religion as that justification. We can also learn that religions survive the humans that follow them, so the problem isn't the people—it's the religions themselves. Murdering all the people who currently believe in the hateful and/or violent teachings of the Bible will not solve the problem. Regardless of lives lost, the Bible can be printed and passed down from generation to generation. Rather, the Bible itself needs to be revised or amended: thus, the need for a Third Testament.

6 – TMI, AND TOO FAST

TMI, which stands for "too much information," is a commonly used acronym in today's day and age. When the actual term was coined is unclear, but it's a perfect description of the information age. People used to be able to filter the information the public received. Daily newspapers were distributed, and such papers would house only the reporters' views of the stories they were covering. Nightly television programs were only on at certain times, so people had small windows of opportunity to find out what was going on in the world. Eventually, the internet was invented, but many lacked the patience to wait for a computer to connect to a network and render the images and text in a readable format. In summary, information was provided slowly from a limited number of sources representing a limited number of perspectives.

I was in school when the internet was invented. In the years prior, we learned about historical events from textbooks and the things our teachers told us. Our abilities to check the accuracy of the information we were receiving or to acquire more information on a particular topic were limited. We could go to the library and check out books related to a topic, but we had no quick way to skim through the pages and quickly find what we were looking for. While we were learning about past wars, new wars were being fought. Awful things were happening every day, as they always have, but we didn't necessarily know about them. This absence of information did wonders for limiting widespread panic, but it also limited the acknowledgement of many deserving people. Movies such as *Hidden Figures*, the story of black female mathematicians who made crucial contributions to NASA, are being made these days to cover the parts of history that weren't told in our textbooks. With the dawn of the internet and smart phones, the new status quo is to be over-informed at all times. In a matter of minutes, we can self-diagnose an illness, check the weather, and learn about the wars currently taking place at 2:00 in the afternoon or 3:00 in the morning. All types of information are always readily available.

It is one thing to allow access to information if people choose to seek it out, but it is quite another to bombard them with information they do not need or want, especially at impressionable ages. Many of today's children receive an overabundance of religious information at a young age. Unfortunately, a healthy respect for a child's inability to critically assess the information she receives has not yet been established. Children are taught to believe in Jesus or any other number of gods at the same time they are taught to believe in Santa Claus. Plenty of children will believe in both Mr. Claus and the deity of choice. The viewpoint of the parents is accepted at face value because, most often, no one else is around to offer an alternative viewpoint. Some children have atheistic or agnostic aunts and uncles who can serve as enlightened witnesses and offer different ways of thinking, but they need to be around the children quite often to really have an impact on their beliefs. Contrary beliefs, such as evolution, are not taught until children are school-aged at which point their parents have already had a number of years to bombard them with stories of creationism if they so choose. Given children need their parents' love, not their teachers', the parents' viewpoint is usually the one adopted.

Kids who are manipulated to live their lives according to Christian beliefs, by proxy, learn that they should *not* steal or murder and other ethical values. These are good lessons because they promote the greater good. However, some young children raised in other religions are learning *to* steal and murder. Regardless of what their parents believe, all children desire their love and approval.

When we are young, our parents are the lens through which we see the world, and they are our life support. To get their approval and love and continue to survive, we believe and do what they tell us to. Society needs to acknowledge that you can train a kid to kill or to believe in Santa Claus. If they're young enough, they won't yet have the ability to assess whether or not what you're asking them to do is a good thing; they'll simply want to do what makes you happy. Society at large should also acknowledge that while parents may not be explicitly training their children to kill or hurt people, training them to hate certain people may lead to either later in life. Parents, especially, need to be conscious of what kinds of information they give to an audience that will literally believe everything it hears and might do almost anything to make them happy. On a less dramatic scale, think of how many people married someone their parents wanted them to marry in order to please them, at the expense of their own personal happiness. Or consider those who pushed themselves through medical school, knowing full well that a career in the arts would have led to more personal satisfaction, but their parents would be happier if they became a doctor. Such stories demonstrate just how strong the desire to please one's parents can be. This desire often trumps all else... and for years and years.

Although we all have too much information these days, lessons learned at impressionable ages can often be dramatically more powerful than new information received at an older age. Most of us, even when we don't want and have no logical reason to be, are loyal to our families. In America, it is considered taboo to challenge your family's beliefs or abandon that group of people, making it extremely hard to discredit the things they told you as a kid. So, parents also need to be aware that whatever they teach their children may stick with them forever, despite all evidence to the contrary. What matters is not the *type* of information received but *whom* it comes from and *when*.

While Christian children haven't formed an army to date, we need to be conscious of the fact that they could in the future. There are plenty of beliefs in the Christian faith that promote hatred—of homosexuals, of "loose" women, of people who drink alcohol, and of non-believers, for example. If hatred of "non-believers" brews for too long, it can boil over into a war, as was the case in the Christian Crusades in the 11th century. In another certain sense, a Christian war has been going on for some time now—on people's psyches. There have been plenty of articles published about homosexuals or transgendered people born into religious households killing themselves. These stories fly in the face of the notion that "God never gives us more than we can handle." These family members fail to see that they are killing those who take their own lives by spewing hate, shaming, and/or withholding the love, medical treatments, choices, and any number of basic human rights they need to survive. These Christian families may fail to see that God is not giving those youths more than they can handle, but the family is. Religion can shame people so badly it leads to death by one's own hand. Compassionate, non-shaming information needs to be presented to these youths, as well as people in all walks of life, both religious and non. However, said information will only be as powerful as the people who believe it and act on it.

In this information age, many Christians have learned of shady dealings within the church and begun to see that other people in the world have different, more comforting beliefs. There are atheist groups, but in my eyes, the act of critical thinking is more important than an end state of disbelief in all religions or belief in a different one. It's more important because it shows that challenging the status quo and thinking for one's self is an option we all have at our disposal.

On a large scale, religious beliefs have been accepted as truths based on the number of followers, not on the evidence. No one has a picture of Jesus on her phone because no one alive has seen him. There is no concrete proof that he exists. Isn't it amazing that in a world where each person has too much information, no one has reliable proof of the deity that so many people are fighting to defend?

When Mark Zuckerberg et al founded Facebook and Jack Dorsey et al founded Twitter, they introduced a new "god" to whom we would all have to answer — the public. CBS and NBC could no longer monopolize the power to widely distribute news. Even more power was put in the public's hands with the invention of the camera phone. With cameras and video recording devices in the phones and at the fingertips of nearly every person, your confessional may reach the priest before you arrive at the church parking lot. In the case of the #BlackLivesMatter movement, videos are reaching the courts before police can confess. People no longer get away with crimes for the length of a lifetime, expecting only to answer to God when they die. God is here in the people on earth, and we have to answer now.

Imagine if the story of Mary and Joseph was merely the first documented incidence of a woman cheating on her husband. These days, if your girlfriend or wife winds up pregnant and you haven't had sex with her, you order a paternity test and find out whose baby it is. There were no paternity tests back then. Perhaps Jesus slightly resembled Joseph's best friend, and it always irked him. We've seen the unshakeable grip of denial in romance addicts on TV, so is it that farfetched to believe Joseph convinced himself Mary was telling the truth? That she truly was a virgin and impregnated by a divine being in the sky? Have we never seen a desperate housewife on TV convincing herself that her husband ISN'T cheating on her? No... we have. Mary would not have gotten away with her plea of innocence so easily in 2017.

Let's take it back even further to the supposed beginning of time and the dynamic duo, Adam and Eve. These two are said to have been the start of humanity. Merely having a theory of how we all came to exist does no harm in and of itself. Such theories become harmful when they are disseminated as absolute fact.

In every picture I have seen of Adam and Eve, they are a white couple. How then, if all people came from these two, are there people of all different skin colors and races? Even if Adam and Eve were mixed race, how are there people with the dark skin tones seen in Africa? Conversely, if both Adam and Eve were black, then how are there white people? Likewise, where did the Asian people come from? Also, how are there seven billion people if the world was populated through incest? All scientific research on the subject, both genetic and psychological, which is now available to anyone, would suggest the human race could not have survived several generations of incest. Incest leads to immense psychological issues and can often lead to a wealth of physical problems for the begotten child. Perhaps no one challenged the story of Adam and Eve for centuries because no one had this information yet. Further, the very Bible that claims the story of Adam and Eve also condemns incest. The book of *Leviticus 18:6* reads: "*None of you shall approach any one of his close relatives to uncover nakedness.*" With only one original couple, it would be impossible to populate the world without incest, which God claimed not to condone. One does not need scientific evidence to question the verity of Adam and Eve's story; only common sense is necessary.

Unfortunately, a lot of impressionable people who have been passing religious beliefs down for centuries lack common sense. Personally, I tried to believe religious teachings as a kid, but I couldn't force these beliefs. It seems the beliefs about myself are harder to shake than my beliefs in someone, or something, else. In my twenties, I experienced the trauma of learning what I used to believe as truth was, in fact, not. Life events led me to question my faith, but watching the movie "The Invention of Lying" and subsequently googling the Bible verses and lessons I had been taught in church sealed the deal. I had too much evidence that Christianity was a hoax to go on believing. I had TMI. When I learned that what I had believed about Christianity was untrue, I felt simultaneously relieved and betrayed. The relief was from knowing an angry father figure wasn't actually floating in the sky waiting to punish me. The betrayal had been by my caretakers and youth pastors, who had lied to me.

Step one toward healing the world is to put it through this very trauma — to admit that we've been believing lies for a long time that are merely ideas which cannot be proven true. If the disciples were to go on CNN and tell the world, "we're sorry; we made the whole thing up," people would be furious. The world would initially be traumatized by the disciples' betrayal, but ultimately relieved to finally know the truth. The disciples are long-since deceased, but we can spread the truth ourselves using social media.

While the speed at which information travels these days and the transparency of our lives on social media may seem scary, both are enormous opportunities for social change. They heighten what each of us has always known to be inarguably true: that we are accountable first to each other. To ignore the information we are bombarded with and can access within seconds would be a bottleneck to our very evolution. We owe it to ourselves, and to each other, to share and use this information. We now have the ability to connect with any number of people and band together to effect social change that benefits the greater good. What we have yet to do on a unified front, however, is to agree on what constitutes the greater good.

On a broad scale, generations before us accepted the greater good as defined by religious texts. This acceptance led to many truly beneficial things but also to sexual abuse, hate crimes, bigotry, sexism, homophobia, racism, and genocide, to name a few. The massive amount of pain these books have caused, and continue to cause, proves that the concept of a greater good cannot be found within them. Such a concept cannot be defined in any book, no matter how old it is or how many people have read it. I fully acknowledge that the greater good is not within my book, either. It is within us, and now, with the power of social media, we know who "us" is.

Pictures, articles, and opinions documenting every type of human experience and habitat are available to everyone within seconds. Those who proclaim on Facebook that they love God are often the ones he has been kind to, such as the able-bodied who can see and are employed. As much as we might not like to, we must acknowledge that some have easier lives on this planet than others. Those who have working legs and can walk around have easier lives than those bound to wheelchairs. Those who can see have an easier life than the blind. Those who have more money typically have less stressful lives than the homeless. The evidence of "who has it good" and "who has it rough" is available online and in real life and is impossible to ignore.

No matter how good or how rough our situation, we're also aware that we are not the only ones in that situation. Oppressed homosexuals living in a Baptist community and females living in extremely sexist religious communities can now feel less alone because they know supportive others are out there, even if they can't see them in person. Did you ever consider that, if god dwells within us, he also dwells within Mark Zuckerberg and Jack Dorsey and compelled each of them to create their social media platforms to further the greater good?

Without an external god to guide us towards what is right, we are forced to look internally for what *feels* right. I believe our natural human reactions and emotions are enough to guide us toward our higher selves and the greater good. People are sharing information online to invoke reactions and emotions, which will inspire people to care and help each other — and it's working. God is not reaching out to us from the sky; god is reaching out from within us and through social media.

7 – NOBODY'S PERFECT, NOT EVEN GOD

Christians believe in an all-knowing, all powerful, all-loving god who never makes mistakes. But, to explain our varied human existences, one has to agree that at least one of those adjectives does not accurately describe god. It is not possible for a perfect, loving god to have created and still co-exist with so much pain and suffering.

After testing into the gifted program in my elementary school, I was told by my parents, "You are smarter than both of us put together. There is nothing you can't do." However, fearing my ego would inflate to unmanageable proportions, they refused to tell me my IQ score. I also remember learning *Ephesians 5:22-24* in church and being confused as to why God would have put such a tremendously capable brain in my female body. As the scripture reads: *Wives, submit to your own husbands, as to the LORD. For the husband is the head of the wife even as Christ is the head of the church, his body, and is himself its Savior. Now as the church submits to Christ, so also wives should submit in everything to their husbands.* I combined this with the lesson from *First Timothy 2:11-12,* and it was very clear to me that God did not want me using this intelligent brain that *he* put in my head. Why would he give me a tool I wasn't supposed to use?

As with all scriptures, there is no fine print in this passage. So according to the scripture, even if I marry a mentally retarded male who is incapable of making sound financial decisions and taking care of his health, I am to submit to him, for he is the head of me. Say I marry an intelligent man instead, but I am having a health problem with my female reproductive organs. Am I to submit to his decision about organs he doesn't have, knowing full well that I'm the one who knows exactly where it hurts and, most likely, why I'm having these symptoms in the first place? You see in the scripture that it says, "submit to their husbands in everything," so if I follow that rule then I have to do what my husband says even if it's the wrong move. Even if I know it's going to kill me, or ruin my chances of happiness, and that I would've made the better choice if I had thought for myself, I have to do what he says. Using the Bible as a guide to live your life can, thus, be a very dangerous endeavor.

If you believe that God is perfect, then wouldn't it make more sense for God to put my brain in a man, where it could be used? Did he make a mistake? Devout Christians will tell you that it is not possible god made a mistake because god is perfect. One could argue god simply put this brain in my body because he intended for me to never marry. I would counter and ask why he would give me a brain so powerful it could question his very existence and a will so strong it could disseminate my thoughts to a widespread audience via this book. I may never marry; time will tell. However, I can tell you for sure that there are plenty of women who *are* married and capable of making better decisions than their husbands. To waste powerful brains merely because they are put in female bodies is hogwash.

God's less palatable mistake, of which we all try not to think, is creating children who die young or are born with a birth defect. If god loves his children, why would he give some of them six or fewer years, filled entirely with pain and spent in an oncology unit of a hospital, to live? If god is perfect and loving, why wouldn't he give all children the same opportunities for happiness and long life? Why has he allowed mass murderers, such as Charles

Manson, to live to be eighty years old and marry multiple times? The only logical conclusions are that god is real but makes mistakes, or that he's not real. Even if there were a real god who makes mistakes, it wouldn't be the god in whom Christians believe. This is not to say children born in less than perfect health and physical form are mistakes — far from it. We cannot, however, deny that a child who can walk has fewer struggles in life than a child who cannot walk. These struggles are given to them by no human, but some people believe a god gave them to the children.

If God's plan was to have everyone believe in Jesus and then bring them home to heaven for all eternity to worship him, then why did he put people in countries far away from those who practice Christianity? These people can be killed before a Christian ever gets there to tell them about Jesus and pray the salvation prayer with them. This implies god either intended to send some people to hell from the get-go (remember he's all-knowing, according to Christians), or yet again, he made a mistake and put them on the wrong continent (he's not perfect). Loving parents will tell you they want the best for their child, and I can guarantee you "the best" does not mean "a fiery inferno for all eternity." Therefore, god can't be all loving if he's knowingly sending some of his children to hell. If god is all-powerful and can send everyone to heaven instead of hell, but still chooses to send some to hell, then he's not all-loving. Given the state of the world we live in, it is not possible for god, or anyone, for that matter, to be simultaneously all-loving, all-powerful, all-knowing, and perfect.

If god makes mistakes, he is flawed. If he is flawed, then he needs our help in running our lives. If he is not real, then we MOST CERTAINLY need to run our own lives: that truth remains unchanged. It's rather scary to be leaving things entirely up to a being who dealt you a shitty hand in the first place and may make more mistakes, putting more roadblocks in your way as you try to make the most of it. The fate of mankind and the world we live in is in our hands now, regardless of whether it was there all along or god passed it to us. Praying to him will not fix our problems, regardless of whether they were god's mistakes or ours. We need to lean on each other.

8 – HOW TO LOSE YOUR RELIGION

When I gave up my belief in a perfect god, I gave up my religion. There's a saying among friends from the support group I sometimes attend: "Religion is for those who don't want to go to hell. Spirituality is for those who have already been there." In my case, this was absolutely true. I lost my religion after I went through my own personal hell, and I've been trying to cultivate my spirituality ever since.

As humans, we tend to care more deeply about things when they directly affect us or our loved ones. While we may be saddened by tragedies happening across the world, we typically do not feel the call to action unless the event affects us personally. When we experience a personal tragedy, most of us feel either the profound presence of something outside ourselves or profoundly alone. During mine, I felt alone. While I didn't truly feel god's love for me as a child, I still believed in and feared him. I didn't fully question his existence until my early twenties, when a close relative developed a problem with alcohol. Although I physically survived this tumultuous time in my life, my belief that a divine father figure loved me and was protecting my family from harm did not.

When I learned that this relative's drinking had progressed to blackouts and vomiting, I realized the seriousness of the situation and got to work to solve the problem. I researched alcohol addiction and treatment options, and I called family members to let them know what was going on. Several of them told me they would "be praying for us"; others came to visit and offer support. During the whole ordeal, I prayed to a god, who I wasn't sure existed, asking that he fix everything. But with each prayer and each passing day, things got worse. I realized at this particular juncture that it is not possible for a god to answer everyone's prayers. If he were real, he would have to be a selective listener. For example, every time there is a sporting event or a job up for grabs, there can be two Christians praying for different outcomes. Each person would want to be the one that got the job, and each team would want the opposing team to lose. God can't answer one's prayer without ignoring the other's. Therefore, it is pointless to pray about these situations because it could lead you to believe God loves others more than you.

It's also pointless to pray to God if you truly believe he is omniscient and all powerful. If you believe such a thing, you would think he already knows what you want, so you do not have to ask him for it. If he truly does know what you want, it's kind of humiliating that he's forcing you to beg for it. True love should feel warm, as if the other person cares about your well-being. Begging for your needs and wants to be met does not feel that way.

After many unanswered prayers, my family staged an intervention and eventually checked this person into a rehab facility. In the midst of my relative's madness, I was in my own personal hell. I went to an outpatient surgery by myself, scared to death I'd get cancer if I didn't, and I didn't even tell my family about it. They were useless as a support system because they were all too fragile and focused on the alcoholic to help me. My boyfriend at the time was also severely emotionally abusive, so throughout this period I had no one to lean on or offer me support. I attempted to tell myself it'd be okay and encourage myself, but I didn't do well.

For three months, I barely slept. My physician expressed concern for my physical safety and prescribed Ambien, a sleeping medication. Even while on the medication, I couldn't sleep one night and had a panic attack at 2:00 a.m. My heart was pounding out of my chest, and I couldn't take in a full breath. Convinced I might be going into cardiac arrest and near death, I walked to the ER—alone. My parents stayed on the phone with me as I walked to and from the hospital, calling periodically to check in while I underwent testing. As I learned that night, the feeling of being alone in a crowded room pales in comparison to feeling alone in an ER. I can still remember the warmth of the iodine the doctors pumped through my veins to check for blood clots at my mother's suggestion. She believed my birth control had created a blood clot in my lungs, which was causing my breathing problems. I suppose it was easier for her to believe it was an entirely physiological problem that had nothing to do with the current tragedy of the family than to believe the truth. The truth was that my family had emotionally abandoned me, the alcoholic was drinking so much that death was a possibility, and, as a result, I was so scared I couldn't breathe.

Months later, my anxiety finally gave way. I accepted that my relative could die any day from addiction, and I was powerless to stop it. I cried in a friend's arms for an entire day, then slept for almost forty-eight hours. Confronted by my brokenness, the alcoholic's brokenness, and the waves of pain crashing into our entire family, I was fully convinced there was no god.

This person did eventually stop drinking, but only after job loss and racking up enough debt that the house needed to be sold. The Christians in my family, of course, quickly jumped to claim that God is good and had cured the addiction. None of the Christians had answers to my questions: If God was truly the one who cured the addict, then why didn't he do so sooner? Why did so many things have to fall apart before he stepped in? Were we the butt of a cosmic joke? Even if God were real, he had just proved I can't count on him for help. He sure as heck wasn't who my family and church said he was. When this relative stopped drinking and I, literally and figuratively, came up for air, I didn't bring my religion with me. That's when I stopped believing in the Christian God, but also any other gods.

This book, and my existence, are physical evidence that not everything is part of a perfect god's plan. The series of events I went through were so severe I turned my back on a god I once believed in. An all-knowing, all-powerful, perfect, unconditionally loving, heavenly father figure, who wants people to believe in him and brings them home to heaven, would not have a plan that involves breaking his own daughter's (Christians believe all of us, including me, are children of God) trust beyond repair. He would know it was going to happen and do something to prevent it. He didn't, however. Not only did I stop believing in him, but I also decided to share my story with as many people as I can. This may result in even fewer people believing in God, and that can't be part of the Christian god's plan. See? He either made a mistake when he gave me this brain, or he's not real.

Throughout this addiction fiasco, I had been communicating with God via prayer. My relationship with God ended because of his lack of reciprocal communication. There has never been a voice from the sky that responds to my questions or requests when I pray. He's never come into my room and physically held me when I told him I was lonely.

All marriage counselors will tell you the most important thing in any relationship is communication. It has to be frequent, tangible, and two-sided. Without that type of communication one or both parties can't tell what the other is thinking or feeling, winds up dissatisfied, and eventually wants out. To illustrate my point, let's use an example. Say your husband never calls you back nor actually speaks to you, so you're forced to try to interpret random coincidences (e.g., sunshine and blooming flowers) as "signs" that he loves you. Would you view that marriage as a healthy relationship? If when you tell him you want to be held, he tells you that he "is already there," but doesn't actually come home from the office, would that satisfy your needs? If you leave that husband who wouldn't talk to you or come see you, is that really your loss? Is it really a loss to you if ANY of your relationships end because the other person won't speak or show up? In my opinion, the answer to all four questions is "no." I lost my religion, but it doesn't feel like a loss to me. I'm not looking to find it again, either.

It was scary to lose my religion. For a time, I feared that I could be wrong and sent to hell for the sin of blasphemy. Then, I remembered a belief in hell was part of the religion I was giving up. As I peeled back the cover of each belief (heaven, hell, salvation, and everything in between) I had previously held, searching for truth, I found that the only way to make the journey less scary was to find strength in numbers. I wanted to see how many other people didn't believe in these concepts either. It was easier to believe I could be right about Christianity being a hoax with each new person I found who had the same thoughts. And at the very least, I'd have some good company in hell if we were all wrong!

It is difficult to challenge a long-standing tradition unless you have strength in numbers. Given the invention of social media, we now have an enormous opportunity to find that strength. I can say from personal experience that merely finding people on Twitter and Facebook who think as you do—even if you never connect with them offline—can be incredibly validating and empowering. For example, I follow Atheist Republic on Facebook but have never spoken to or met any of the members. However, just knowing that there are over one million people who belong to the group helped give me permission to be who I truly am and feel how I truly feel. I am writing this book in hopes that anyone who is hiding among the religious, wondering if it's okay to step away, disagree with their teachings, and never look back, will see that it is. You're not the only one who has ever thought that way. Like me, you may be the "odd one out" in your current situation, but you won't be the odd one out in every situation. The more you speak up, the more that "one out" can become "two out," "three out," and so on, until we're all thinking for ourselves.

9 – NOT ALL WARS INVOLVE GUNS

One inarguable truth is that we cannot hurt another without also hurting ourselves. In the same way your fist will hurt if you punch a face, you will feel a pang of guilt if you say something mean and hurt someone's feelings. The harm need not be physical to be felt by both parties, and the experience of that pain is characteristically human—not Christian, male, Caucasian, etc. A less widely accepted truth is that hurtful words can cause as much pain, if not more, as a gunshot wound.

In the past several years, I learned disturbing things about family histories from people I know. Addiction, child abuse, suicide attempts, and molestation have all been recounted to my no-longer-virgin ears.

These dark subjects are no longer separate from me on the silver screen at a movie theater but have actually affected the lives of me and my loved ones. Though no one I know has taken a gun or weapon and killed someone, it is clear that generations before me waged a war. Unable to retaliate against their perpetrators (a.k.a., parents), due to the family history of belief in the fifth commandment, each waged an emotional war on the next generation. The pent-up feelings of anger and distress from verbal and/or physical lashings during one's own childhood are potent and cannot be suppressed for an entire lifetime. These feelings are often released onto the next generation of innocent children who, due to the fifth commandment, are also not allowed to fight back.

Typically, if someone accidentally steps on your toe and hears you cry out in pain, that person will jump off your toe immediately and apologize. Similarly, if a person is at all compassionate and sees you crying because of something they said, they will apologize or try not to say it again, so they do not have to see you in distress. The basic instincts after having caused pain are guilt and remorse. These basic instincts are not allowed to be acted upon in the homes of religious fanatics due to the belief that the teachings of the Bible trump basic human instinct. In a dysfunctional family, each new parent believes they do not have to take their children's feelings seriously because their own parents did not take theirs seriously. Pain or tears were not regarded as signals for the parents to stop screaming at or spanking their children, so they, in turn, do not stop hurting their own children when they cry out.

Although I was never physically abused, beating children is condoned in the Bible, which led to some of my friends and relatives being beaten in their religious homes. *Proverbs 13:24* reads: *Whoever spares the rod hates his son, but he who loves him is diligent to discipline him.* Some religious fanatics who believe everything in the Bible is truth actually believe they NEED to beat their children to show them they love them because of this verse!

As a Christian, I wasn't allowed to believe my parents were to blame for my suffering. The scripture taught me to honor them and believe everything they did for me or to me came from love. Likewise, I was not allowed to blame God for my pain because he was believed to be omnipotent, omnipresent, and loving. No matter what happened in my life, I was instructed to believe it was a part of "God's" plan. Additionally, because my hurt feelings often didn't change the way my family members or the church leaders treated me, I started to believe I deserved to be hurt. Harboring intense anger at my circumstances, with no allowable place to put blame, I put it on myself. I believed my parents were justifiably mean and neglectful because I was a bad, unlovable kid. It was the only remaining explanation.

While not encouraging people to shoulder the blame for childhood abuse they have suffered, most therapists and support groups discourage their clients and members from blaming the parents. Society at large absolves parents of all guilt for child abuse, corroborating their story that they "did the best they could, passing on what was done to them without knowing any better." I was taught that my parents and grandparents didn't have support groups for people to heal their own childhood traumas and treat their children better. While that may be true, I also know that the support group I routinely go to was created by people my parents' age. Rather than accept that they didn't have resources, some people in that age group created them. From my perspective, my parents could have done the same thing. The people that created the support groups chose to think outside the box, acknowledge their own pain, and learn how to prevent it in future generations, rather than use those generations to avenge it. For those who didn't find or create support groups prior to having children, therapy was still an option at the time. From my perspective, parents who did not seek enough therapy or divorce each other once they became miserable did not do the best they could. They simply upheld the status quo.

In 2017, women can choose not to get married or have children until they are sure their emotional wounds from childhood (if any) have healed and that they will not harm anyone. My grandparents did not have the same freedom to choose whether or not to have children, and how many, because birth control options were limited. My grandmothers also had less freedom to choose whether or not to get married than I do today because opportunities for female financial independence were limited. However, the freedom I have today came from women in previous generations who fought for the rights I have rather than simply birthing children and passing on the dysfunction. While some grandmothers may think they did the best they could, in my opinion, the grandmothers who fought for those rights did better. With these rights comes responsibility.

Thanks to the widespread availability and affordability of various forms of birth control, people now need to be held responsible for when, whether, and how many children they have. Potential parents are responsible for considering their financial abilities to support a child, as well as their emotional capabilities to support the child's healthy development. My family was financially stable, and I never went without food, shelter, or clothing. However, we were spiritually and emotionally poor, from my perspective, and it severely stunted my emotional development. Over the years, I have sat in meeting rooms with my support group, across from people raised by poor and/or physically abusive parents, even though mine were neither. And yet, we share the same emotional handicaps. The effects of deficient parenting can be lifelong and are highly contagious, regardless of the type of deficiency.

If people aren't held accountable for how they treat their kids, especially by their own children, things will continue to get worse. Actions without consequence will be repeated. This is why our bodies get fat and our health deteriorates when we eat too much food. Without these negative consequences, a lot of people would never stop eating. Likewise, if people let their parents get away with child abuse with no negative feedback, the parents will continue to abuse them. If they don't hold their parents accountable for their pain, they're more likely to hold, unfairly, their own children accountable instead. There needs to be a negative consequence to stop the cycle. That consequence is the placement of blame for child abuse where it belongs—on the parents' shoulders.

We, as human beings, are not simply victims of the time in which we live, incapable of change. Susan B. Anthony was alive at a time when women could not vote, and she sought to make it happen. She didn't accept the world the way in which it was handed to her, planning to tell her children, "that's the way it was back then." Martin Luther King, Jr. didn't accept racial inequality and plan to tell his children that he didn't fight for equal rights because, "That's just the way it is. I did the best I could." Each of us can choose to listen to our true feelings and fight for the rights that are being trampled on. We are accountable for whether we make that choice or not. Each of us is responsible for not waging a war on the next generation—guns or no guns. We need to declare a ceasefire on emotional abuse.

10 – WHEN IS DAD COMING HOME, AND WHEN IS GOD COMING HOME?

Devout Christians prepare all their lives for "The Second Coming," which they believe to be a day when Jesus will return to Earth, take all the good people to heaven, and cast all the bad people into hell. These Christians will also tell you that they very much look forward to this day because they are certain they will be in the group going to heaven. These people are literally sitting around with bated breath, ready to jump at a moment's notice to do whatever someone who abandoned them thousands of years ago wants them to do. However, in present times, the triumphant return of an earthly father after a prolonged absence is often not an event to be celebrated.

Think of someone whose father abandoned her the day she was born, only to pop back into her life much later. The story of her father's return is never peaceful, and the child in the situation does not just drop everything to do whatever Dad wants to do. No self-respecting person would. The first question upon his return is, "Where *were* you?" The second is, "Why weren't you here all along?" I imagine it's scary for people who have devoted their entire lives to the Christian faith to consider the possibility of resentment, rather than joy, on the day of the hypothetical Second Coming. It may frighten them to ask themselves, "How will I actually feel if that day comes while I'm still alive?" "If I am seated at the right hand of the father, slated to go to heaven, would I really want to go with him?" And "Why did he leave me in the first place?"

Imagine if people believed Jesus was going to come back a second time but this time as a woman. My church taught us that Jesus came back as a man, and I find it unsurprising that a widespread patriarchy prevailed after this alleged divine visitation. It seems to me that Jesus only successfully understood the male perspective and then made sure they had everything they wanted. Women have been fighting tooth and nail for what they want, deserve, and need for decades. I see no reason for females to worship a mythical man who failed to represent them and is not here to help them now.

It wasn't until recently that I connected the dots between the story of the second coming and my strained relationship with my own earthly father. He worked long hours, and as a result, one of the things he and Jesus had in common was that I never knew when either of them was coming home. In my early years, I would try to stay up as late as I could in hopes that I'd see him. Then I got used to him being gone and started to resent him, so I'd pretend to be asleep when he got home. I didn't know how to express how abandoned and insignificant he made me feel. I also thought expressing these feelings would be unfair because it would mean I was holding him to a higher standard than that to which I was told to hold Jesus himself. If no Christian expected Jesus to be here now, they certainly wouldn't expect my father to be here now, so neither should I. Thus, my father became unaccountable to me. I now fully understand the message I absorbed in childhood: "Men only need to be there when they want to be, and you better drop everything and come running when they are."

As the years went on, I continued to accept crumbs of attention from my father. I'd get brief phone calls every month or so, and I'd see him a few times a year, but usually only if I travelled home. For nearly ten years I've lived in a city that is a one-hour plane ride from his home. It wasn't until I bought my own house and he refused to come see it without my estranged mother that everything clicked. He doesn't feel the need to come see me for me to keep loving him and keep a "relationship" with him. Clearly, the alleged Jesus feels the same as my father does.

My first relationship with a man was with my father and my second with God. Therefore, what I had been conditioned to accept from both became what I accepted from all men. Looking at my relationship history, I see that I dated what I was familiar with — distant men. I dated workaholics, exercise addicts, and alcoholics, all of whom picked different poisons but shared a common goal: absence.

Just like I didn't know how to hold my father to a higher standard than my god, I didn't know how to hold my boyfriend to a higher standard than my own father. I didn't feel I could expect my boyfriend to spend more time with me when my own father chose not to spend time with me. I also couldn't get mad at him without feeling my suppressed rage at my father, and I didn't want to go there. When my dad finally chose not to come visit me in my thirty-first year of life, I was forced to face my rage. An important decision accompanied said rage. I decided that if I am going to respect myself in one relationship, I have to respect myself in all of them. I can't make an exception and allow one person to treat me poorly but not all the others. I could no longer allow my father to not show up for me and simultaneously dump my boyfriend for the same reason. Both relationships had to break. The issue is the behavior (i.e., not showing up), not who does it. Parental status does not exempt someone from being an asshole. To truly comprehend this lesson that I learned, you really have to get outside the status quo, which is to maintain your relationship with your parents no matter what.

My father was capable of spending more time with me than he did when I was a child. He's self-employed and sets his own hours. He has always had his own car and enough money to pay for gas or plane tickets. Hell, he could be here right now, sitting across from me on the couch as I write this. But he's not —because he *chooses* not to be. My father is a human... someone who is not omnipotent, all powerful, and all-knowing. If he is able to physically be here and only has earthly means to get here, we KNOW Jesus could be here, too. After all, people believe he revived himself from the grave; a quick trip back to earth should be a piece of cake.

The lesson that your own father *can* be there for you but *chooses* not to be is, admittedly, a very hard pill to swallow. It hurts because we are taught all our lives that parents always love and prioritize their children more than anyone in the world ever could. We hear stories of parents' hearts "exploding with the most all-consuming love you could ever imagine" in the delivery room as their children are born, but we have no memory of whether our own parents actually felt that way. Because of this lesson, we define love as the way our parents treat us. As a kid trying to make sense of why my parents told me they loved me but still made me feel lonely and forgotten, I just decided love wasn't supposed to make you feel good. As I grew older, I met men who showed me love by making me feel good; they made an effort to be around me consistently. Unfortunately, I still needed to believe that my dad loved me more than they did, so I pushed them away. If any of you are reading this, I'm sorry — you know who you are. I literally had to be completely alone or surrounded by people who made me feel unimportant for my father's love to be better in comparison. This led to my phase of long-distance relationships and relationships with military men, who are the only men that seemed less available than my dad had been.

The time during which I needed my father around most has passed. My childhood is over, so I'm left with the decision of what to do if he finally chooses to be around me and build a closer relationship with me. My brain has been crammed with societal agendas from childhood through adulthood about what I am supposed to do. The phrase "they're family" is supposed to excuse all manner of sins. I'm expected to keep the proverbial door open to him for life and allow him to walk right back through when he decides to show up, no matter when or how infrequent that may be. But regardless of what I'm expected to do, ultimately, I will decide whether to keep the door open for his "second coming".

One of the key problems in dysfunctional families is that the members believe the phrase: "We're family — we stick together through everything" implies an obligation, rather than a desire. Some of my family members have treated me and each other worse than most people I've met and am not related to because they believed that no matter what they did to the family, they had to stick around. It wasn't until my late twenties that I finally told my own family, "Families shouldn't stick together because they have to, but because they want to. The people who do stick by their families feel so loved by them that they can't imagine being anywhere else." By that point I didn't feel loved by many of them, so I wanted to be anywhere else. Plenty of people imply, rather than say, this by moving far, far away from their families and rarely calling home.

I often think how much easier it would be to process my feelings if society didn't expect me to give my family endless chances to be better. I think of the great friends I have in my life who have never, and would never, dream of hurting me in the ways my family has. They don't need endless chances to be better because they haven't ruined the first one. There will be no "second coming" for them because they haven't abandoned me in the first place. These friendships are not a struggle because trust has been gained and never broken beyond repair. We spend quality time together, and remorse is expressed immediately if feelings are hurt. I'm even writing this book in hopes that some of you can help create a society in which we are not expected to sustain all types of relationships, be they familial, romantic, professional, or otherwise, that lack trust. Our current society only approves of parental or familial estrangement in the case of incest. Even then, some extreme right-wing Christians would have the victims forgive their transgressors and let them back in their lives, believing they are fostering Christ-like character in the victims.

I believe victims of abuse think deep down that maybe only God can love their perpetrators unconditionally because God was not the victim of the abuse. For example, I have to wonder if roles were reversed and someone molested Jesus in his childhood, would God still be able to forgive and love that person unconditionally? There are plenty of people who love abusive parents but are not related to them, but would they be able to do so if they had been the abused child? It's a lot easier to forgive someone for their crime if that crime wasn't against you or your child.

I don't believe everyone on earth deserves unconditional love and forgiveness from every other person, but I also don't think that's a bad thing. I believe this because there are over seven billion people in the world. If a person is born into a group of people or marries someone that humiliates and abuses her on a regular basis, I believe she needs to leave and find other people whose conditions through which she needs to love them are not so unforgivable. There is a difference between someone who accidentally answers "yes" when a woman asks if a dress makes her look fat once and someone who says, "you are worthless and lucky to have a relationship with any man at all" every day. The first transgression is forgivable; the second is unforgivable, and bags should be packed to leave. With no divine father figure here to save her, she needs to take care of herself.

Jesus, like many of our fathers, still hasn't shown up. Given all the help the people in the world currently need, it's clear that he should have come back by now to take care of us. We all need to stop waiting for him, or any other fatherly figure, to come back and help us. Just because we think someone *should* show up for us, perhaps because he's our father or she's our mother, doesn't mean that person will. Instead, we need to respect ourselves and surround ourselves with the people who choose to be around us now.

11 – WHY DOES GOD PREFER ME TO STAY MARRIED RATHER THAN HAPPY?

Christians who follow the rules of the Bible in a literal sense can spout off any number of verses that describe God's feelings about divorce. One verse says he hates it; another describes ex-spouses as adulterers if they marry other people, etc. The sum total of the messages is usually preached to churchgoers as "divorce is bad, so don't get one, no matter what happens to you." Dutiful Christians may follow the rules and live most of their lives unhappily tied to a person who makes them miserable. Viewing God's happiness with them as more important than their own happiness, they will consider their life a success.

Personally, I don't believe it is more important to follow rules than to be truly happy and respect yourself. All humans make mistakes, and a common mistake, as evidenced by the roughly 50% divorce rate these days, is marrying the wrong person. If you marry the wrong person for you at age twenty-two and your life expectancy is eighty-two, common sense would say it's far better to divorce this person, as soon as you're certain of the mistake, than to stay with him. Then you'll be able to live as many happy years as you can, rather than spending sixty years being miserable. I can tell you from personal experience that parents who won't divorce, and fight like cats and dogs, can be just as damaging to their children as parents who do divorce. Since either outcome will negatively affect their children, they might as well choose the option that leads to the most happiness for themselves. Then, they'll be modelling self-respect, rather than martyrdom, for their children. This also teaches children to find happiness within themselves, which is a vital skill for healthy self-esteem.

My parents screamed, yelled, slammed doors, threw dishes, and stormed out of the house in front of us as children. They also claimed to be madly in love with each other the whole time, have been married more than thirty-five years, and, I believe, will never get divorced. As a result, I have severe trouble with relationships because a healthy fight and the resolution of its cause was never modeled for me as a child. My parents, by example, defined love as chaos and pain. A relationship was modeled as a series of saves from destruction rather than a steady flow of peace. This deeply engrained definition of love often leads me to avoid it altogether, too. If love is pain, and I don't want to be in pain, then I figure I would really rather not be in love.

By growing up in a chaotic environment, I also never learned when to leave an uncomfortable situation. While he didn't divorce my mother, my father did leave her by working as much as possible. Meanwhile, my mother loudly complained about how unhappy she was with my father because of his absence but tried to explain that she was staying with him for us (her children). In other words, she was a martyr blaming all of us for her unhappiness. What we learned was that her happiness, or that of anyone else who is in a relationship, doesn't matter, and that no matter how bad it gets, you shouldn't leave.

The status quo is that hardly anyone will fault you for divorcing your spouse if she beats you, molests your child, or is unfaithful to you. None of these reasons applied in my family, so I think my parents had a harder time finding a reason to split up. I know now that if a relationship causes me MUCH more misery than peace, and I've tried working it through but nothing changes, then

I should leave and find another one. I wish my parents had come to the same realization, for my sake and their own.

Personally, I don't believe in a god that wants a person to stick to a promise made on his wedding day, which has since made him miserable, more than he wants him to be happy. Think of it this way: if your spouse beats you and molests your child, and you believe God wants you to stay with her no matter what, then you believe God wants you to be beaten and your child to be molested. If that's the case, then what kind of sick god do you believe in? Abuse and incest is not love, and no truly loving person or deity would wish that fate on anyone. In fact, no loving person would want you to be deeply unhappy, which you no doubt would be in such a marriage.

If you set all your pre-conditioning aside, the concept I'm addressing in this chapter should be pretty easy to grasp. It is two-fold: 1) pursue what makes you happy, be it a marriage, a career, a car, a long jog, etc., and 2) leave or avoid what makes you miserable and unhealthy. The decision of what to pursue and what to avoid has nothing to do with the person, place, or thing itself and everything to do with how you feel about it. Given each person has a unique personality and set of likes and dislikes, people, places, and things will not evoke the same universal feelings from every person. Depending on the feelings prompted by each, certain people should pursue them and others avoid them.

To convince people to ignore their feelings, universally approach certain things (e.g., marriage), and avoid others (e.g., divorce), the Christian church invented the concept of heaven and hell. Heaven is the ultimate delayed gratification. One Christian belief, in a nutshell, is: "you may feel miserable in this current life, but as long as you follow the rules, you will forever be happy in heaven after you die." I would love to ask people who believe this message, "If God wants you to be forever happy, then why doesn't he want you to be happy now?" Think of St. Jude's fundraisers or Susan G. Komen walks for breast cancer. The idea behind these events is to raise money for a better future for sick children and women. Even though a cure for cancer has not yet been found, women and children are still using chemotherapy and experimental treatments. A loving person wants to ease their present discomfort AND improve their future (give a better life today AND tomorrow). Likewise, although a person may not yet have found a new loving spouse, he or she can still leave the abusive one and ease the present discomfort.

Staying in an abusive relationship or other awful situation helps neither party in said predicament. Anyone who stays with an abusive spouse hopes that he will eventually stop abusing her. However, just as no one can stop an alcoholic from abusing a substance, other than himself, no one can stop a person from abusing another person, other than himself. Staying with that person will not stop the abuse and may, in fact, prolong it. Spouses who stay in abusive relationships become enablers. They shield the perpetrator from experiencing any negative consequences of his actions (in this case, abandonment) and, thus, remove any motivation for him to change.

I have focused a lot on physical and sexual forms of abuse in this chapter, merely because it is easiest to drive home a point with these types of examples. From personal experience, I can tell you that emotional and religious abuse is just as insidious as the other forms. I believe emotional abuse is also grounds for divorce or separation, especially when children are involved. Emotional abuse is an example of classical, albeit fucked up, conditioning. In the same way you can train a dog to stay in its cage, you can train a human to stay in its relationship. Emotional abuse convinces a person to stay by making her believe she can't, or doesn't deserve to, leave and find a better situation. Emotional wounds are arguably even harder to heal than physical wounds because they do not automatically invoke sympathy from others. If someone sees a bruise on your face from where your spouse hit you, they will likely instantaneously express concern and offer to help. People cannot see wounds on your heart and mind, though, which requires you to voice them to invoke sympathy and help from others. It's also much easier to straighten a broken bone than a broken thought process. Healing times are unpredictable and impossible to track when the wound is emotional.

As an unmarried person, I am somewhat baffled by the concept of making a lifelong commitment. Alcoholics are not encouraged to quit alcohol once and for all, but, rather, one day at a time. This is because "once and for all" is likely an impossible promise to keep. Alcoholics are, therefore, encouraged to quit "one day at a time" because that is what is achievable. It is not possible for them to predict all the circumstances for the rest of their lives that may make them want to drink. It is, however, possible to make a choice not to drink today and to make that same choice tomorrow. Similarly, I don't see how it's possible to commit to be faithful to and love one person for the rest of your life. Upon making this promise, you have no idea whether you will want to cheat on him thirty years down the road (or him on you), whether he will take up shooting heroin into his arm and sell your house for drug money, etc. Therefore, I will likely only promise to commit to a man one day at a time. I could only feasibly see myself entering into a marriage after we both agree to divorce if it becomes unhealthy, or perhaps for tax benefits. Life ebbs and flows, and sustaining rigid beliefs that may no longer hold true (e.g., we love each other and we're both being responsible for ourselves) does neither of us any good. In fact, commitment without love can feel much worse than being single because it's loneliness COUPLED with rejection. I have no problem with the institution of marriage and admire people who enter into it believing they will, at least, try to stay together forever. I just also believe these people should be allowed to divorce if the marriage comes to cause more pain than joy.

12 – EXPECTING HUMANS TO DO THINGS ONLY A GOD COULD DO

A key goal of a Christian life, as taught to me by the churches I grew up in, is to be Christ-like in all one's endeavors. Since this is not possible, due to human emotions and inherent imperfections, such a lifestyle can lead to endless feelings of shame and guilt. In the same way that we do not expect a baby to give a speech at a conference, we should not expect adults to do things beyond their capabilities, things only a god could do. The two Christ-like aspirations I will focus on in this chapter are forgiving all your trespassers and loving all your enemies as yourself. We cannot fairly expect people to forgive someone for a transgression, or a sum of transgressions, so terrible or so damaging that only a deity would be able to forgive them. It's also not fair to expect someone to truly love people who are cruel to her—her enemies—no matter their initial biological or relational ties.

If you're looking for ways to get over a painful past, you'll find no shortage of advice telling you to do so by forgiving those who hurt you. Such advice is not entirely unwise and unfounded, but as with any type of advice, it cannot be universally taken. Different circumstances bring about different feelings and decisions, depending on the person. Sometimes, no matter how hard you try, you CAN'T forgive someone for what they did to you. Forgiveness is a feeling, and we cannot force ourselves to have a feeling. Plenty of songs acknowledge that we can't make ourselves love another person, but I haven't heard one that acknowledges we can't force ourselves to forgive another person either.

When something hurtful happens to us, we blame someone. Our mind will be incapable of dealing with the situation without placing blame because it understands that feelings don't happen in a vacuum. Between people, there is cause and effect. If you forgive your trespasser for hurting you, then the only person left to blame is you. This was the route I chose for a long time. I blamed myself for the religious abuse I suffered and attempted to forgive my family for it, excusing them for "not knowing any better" and "not meaning to hurt me." My mental and physical health suffered as a result.

The divorce rate is now climbing past 50% for reasons such as infidelity or even minor "irreconcilable differences." Society is very understanding of the dissolve of marital relationships for minor infractions but often extremely judgmental of the dissolve of biological relationships, no matter the severity of transgressions. My question to society is: If it's that difficult—nay, impossible—to forgive someone who we loved and chose to marry as an adult, for being unfaithful or taking us for granted, why do people expect defenseless children to forgive abuse in relationships they did not choose to enter – with their parents? Typically, the punishment doesn't fit the crime; it fits the perpetrator. A parent and a spouse could commit the same crime against a person (perhaps it's constant verbal abuse), and the spouse will get a life sentence (restraining order and divorce) whereas the parent will get a slap on the wrist.

I would argue that sometimes—maybe even most of the time—forgiveness for abuse is impossible. Regardless of whether it's possible, I am a firm believer that it is not necessary. No matter how hard I try, my heart can't forgive my parents and grandparents for the religious abuse I endured as a child. My brain has impeded forgiveness as well. It can't understand why, when I meet random strangers in my daily life who are kind to me and pursue hanging out with me, I would forgive and force relationships with people who were cruel to me or neglected me for years on end. It's much easier to form relationships with the strangers who don't need my forgiveness for cruel treatment first. I eventually gave up on forgiving my perpetrators and chose to live a life in pursuit of others who are kind to me and actively trying to be emotionally healthy.

If a victim of child abuse cannot forgive her perpetrator, but society has advised that victim to do so, it is adding insult to her injury, or in this case, guilt on top of shame. The child will feel guilty because she cannot forgive, and she will already be feeling shame as a direct result of the abuse. By shaming and blaming herself, the victim creates an illusion that she had control over what happened to her and that she can prevent it from happening in the future. However, the reality is that she couldn't prevent the abuse any more than she can force herself to forgive the abuser; they are both beyond her control. Anger, fight and/or flight are natural responses to being abused, whereas forgiveness is not. If it were, we wouldn't have to read self-help books and pay for therapy to figure out how to do it. The status quo tells us that compassion and forgiveness are the universal keys to moving on, but this ignores the fact that grief and forgiveness, or lack thereof, are entirely personal journeys. While forgiveness may help one person move on, it may hold another back and even make them ill. Only the victim knows whether forgiving the perpetrator is even possible, and if doing so will make her feel better. The status quo of forgiveness being forced on victims of child abuse needs to be replaced with a status quon't: Decide for yourself how you will heal from your trauma and who will be in your life once it's complete.

The severity of a transgression does not determine whether forgiveness is warranted or possible, either. A sum of seemingly endless small slights can be harder to forgive, in aggregate, than one unspeakable act of cruelty. For example, calling someone an "idiot" is generally viewed as a minor offense which is forgivable if done on rare occasions in a fit of anger. However, calling someone an idiot several times a week over many years, especially if that someone is a child, is less forgivable. If you do this to a young child, you will have lowered his self-esteem in potentially irreparable ways. In the same way that we cannot get a song out of our heads if we've heard it too many times, we may not be able to get a belief about ourselves out of our heads if it was repeated to us over and over. I endured constant criticism daily for years until I left home, and although I could easily say the words "I forgive you" to my abuser, I can't make myself mean them. The timeframe and stage of life during which the abuse occurs matters greatly. In my case, the hurtful words were piled on before I was old enough to have a sense of doubt and a solid self-esteem. Had I possessed either of these at the time, perhaps I could have sloughed the criticisms off as untrue— projections of the abuser's own insecurities— rather than valid assessments of my own inadequacies. But since I had neither, I believed I truly was unattractive, as was constantly said, and that I was deserving of constant punishments and criticism.

It's reasonable to expect someone, myself included, to forgive a small, infrequent slight, such as being cut off in traffic. Any number of people might commit this transgression occasionally and even accidentally. It's unreasonable to expect someone to forgive a person for things most people wouldn't do, such as murdering your pet dog, or wouldn't keep doing, such as calling you mean names. From personal experience, I can tell you that it becomes harder to forgive someone for abusing you when you surround yourself with more and more people who don't abuse you. I think one of the reasons there are so many people on earth is so we don't have to forgive and love every single one. The person who abuses you probably does not abuse everyone he knows, so he doesn't necessarily need your forgiveness to get on with his life, either. He, too, can find other people to spend time with. Nobody benefits from a situation in which forgiveness is given from someone who doesn't want to give it to someone who didn't ask for it, doesn't need it, and may not even want it. I hope you can now see that the status quo is not always the best status.

The other Christ-like behavior I view as an ill-advised pursuit is loving your enemies as yourself. A verse from the book of Matthew encourages this pursuit. *Matthew 5:39 But I say to you, do not resist the one who is evil. But if anyone slaps you on the right cheek, turn to him the other also.* Following this advice would be harmful to your health, not only because it's a denial that you deserve better treatment, but also because it could be a threat to your physical safety. These days, if a woman shows up at a shelter with a black eye, the staff will not tell her to return to her husband so he can hit her other eye. The advice given in the book of Matthew is downright stupid. While a supernatural deity may theoretically be able to forgive and survive being slapped around in perpetuity, a human cannot. For a human, this behavior of putting one's self in harm's way is simply unsafe. It's also unwise because it enables the abuser. Having experienced no negative consequences for having hit someone, and in fact being encouraged to keep going when the other cheek is presented, he'll have no reason to stop. The one being slapped around becomes a martyr, the relationship remains unhealthy, and nobody feels better. If the victim does gain some self-respect and leaves, she can also not be expected to forgive the abuser. If she truly wants to forgive and finds it possible, that is one thing, but she may not be able to. Perhaps the trust between them has been broken beyond repair, and she will never feel safe around him again.

Matters of forgiving abuse and loving enemies can surely be hoped for, but it should not be expected. A god may be the only one truly capable of either. Although the status quo would have us believe that forgiveness and love have been granted in these situations, it may have only been spoken, not truly felt.

13 – CONTROL OF BIRTH CONTROL PILLS

Bible verses have been used as the primary arguments for why women should not have access to and use birth control or have abortions, despite no verse in the Bible explicitly saying either. If you read the Bible, you will not find a verse that says, "Women should never have abortions," nor a verse that says, "Women should never try to prevent pregnancy." What you will find is *Psalm 127:3,* a common verse of choice used in a birth control debate. This verse states: *"Behold, children are a heritage from the LORD, the fruit of the womb a reward."*

On a large scale, Bible-thumping has been an attempt to control the use of birth control pills. I cannot understand why people believe the Bible, which was written by men and is hundreds of years old, governs birth control pills and abortions, which are tens of years old and used by women. It is not even possible for rules about birth control or abortion to have existed in the Bible because neither had been invented when it was written. However, conservative Christians seem to be waiting for a new Bible verse or "sign from God" that it's okay to use birth control or have an abortion before they agree with the non-Christians who are already on board with both. Thus, we have found another reason to write a Third Testament – we could include sensical verses about birth control and abortion.

Many conservative Christians are conflicted about types of killing. Some have gone as far as murdering abortion providers. The message sent: "I can kill you, but you can't kill anyone" is both hypocritical and sickening. Even more absurd is that these people claimed to be "pro-life." Such a label would seem to imply supporting all lives, not just those of unborn children. Curiously, many pro-lifers also oppose birth control. They want to prevent the senseless murder of fetuses but are opposing the very pills and devices than can prevent such occurrences in the first place.

Pro-lifers seem to have been waiting a long time for an undeniable sign from God that abortion and birth control are okay. All of the examples of "signs from God" presented in the Bible are explicit—you can't miss them. The sea parted in two before people's very eyes, a man walked on water, water became wine, etc. No one has seen such obvious miracles and received such explicit guidance for hundreds of years (I would argue ever, but alas...), so I'm not sure what people think a sign from God looks like these days. I feel so strongly that birth control should be available to all that I'll even argue from a faith-based standpoint to try to reach the religious folks. So here goes.... what if the mere presence of birth control is a message from God that you should use it? Imagine you are on a deserted island and a boat appears... As a Christian, you would almost certainly see the boat as a gift from God that you are supposed to use to save your life. Consider that we are already on a proverbial island, and the proverbial boat is birth control. Birth control can save lives. Over the years, far too many women have died in childbirth and far too many unwanted children have been abandoned or killed, and the pill is the saving grace from more of that occurring. I hope we can agree to disagree on whether that saving grace came from a god or from scientists, but that we can all agree that regardless of where it came from, it's here and should be used.

Interestingly, Christians do not seem to be waiting for a sign from God that the use of Viagra is permissible.

Plenty of people who identify as pro-life view a woman getting pregnant as God's will but do not view a man being *unable* to get a woman pregnant as God's will. This is a blatant double standard. To be clear, I am not arguing that both Viagra and birth control be outlawed; I am arguing that the debate should end and both be available to all. It is entirely unfair to promote a man's ability to get someone pregnant but not a woman's ability to *not* get pregnant.

Another argument from the Catholic Church against birth control is that if God allows a woman to become pregnant, then he wants that child to be born. The argument is a loose interpretation of *Psalm 127:3*. This belief leads many fanatically religious families to have a child every time they become pregnant and not take measures to prevent future pregnancies. They believe if it happens, no matter when and how often, God intended to give them that child. A free-thinking, logical person can see that it makes absolutely no sense for countless children to be born. If Christians truly believe that God is all-knowing, then they would logically have to believe that he knows some children conceived and born will wind up in incapable, sometimes downright abusive, hands. A truly loving and all-knowing god would, logically, have to support the use of mechanisms (birth control) that ensure children are only conceived when they will be born into loving arms. One famous couple believed that every child they conceived should be born—the Duggars. Given the scandal surrounding this family that surfaced in 2015, it seems some of their children were born into arms that were already too full.

I don't know the Duggar family, personally, so I don't know whether they actually wanted nineteen children or simply believed they had to have them because of their religion. However, if it is the latter.... the situation is unbelievably worse. When a couple has more children than they even want to give love to, the children grow up angry and depressed.

It is not possible for two people to have enough time and energy to share with nineteen other people, especially not evenly and on a consistent basis. In general, marriages are two-person agreements, for this same reason. Having nineteen spouses would not be healthy; someone would feel starved for attention at all times. Even if the Duggar parents were to treat their children entirely equally, the cumulative amount of time each child would get in the end would not be enough to fill a heart with love and support healthy emotional development. For example, if each Duggar parent spent one full day with each child, it could be at least eighteen days until that child received that parent's full attention again. The child would likely have the other parent's full attention somewhere in that eighteen days, but could still wait upwards of a week for it. Having a parent's full attention that infrequently would be considered neglect, by all practical standards.

In a Christian fundamentalist home, children who are starved for adequate attention and love feel guilty about ever expressing their, truly warranted, anger at their parents because of the fifth commandment (honor thy father and mother). The anger does not disappear, however, so it is turned inward until it can later be released, often upon unsuspecting, weaker victims. Josh Duggar's scandal, in which he was caught cheating on his spouse and confessed to molesting his sisters, is an example of this phenomenon. My best guess as to what happened is that Josh was made to feel guilty for his mounting sexual needs during puberty and was denied an outlet for them (i.e. relations with a girlfriend) because of his parents' belief that pre-marital sex is a sin and courtship should be chaperoned. When the sexual desire and/or need became too much for him to bear, he acted out on his unsuspecting sisters. After being starved for adequate parental love and attention, he entered a marriage with an empty love tank, and one person couldn't possibly fill it up, so he cheated on her. Birth control could have helped prevent this outcome. Had the Duggars used birth control to stop having children after they had two or three, they could have potentially raised kids who didn't feel neglected. Because of the size of the religious community, as well as the number of unsuspecting victims it can affect, a lack of birth control would be a societal problem. It would negatively impact the mental and emotional health of not only the children born into religious homes, but also, potentially, everyone they encounter. Therefore, it's dangerous to all of us to even discuss taking away women's rights to birth control, and it saddens me that such discussions are still taking place in 2017.

Incestual rape can also have a ripple effect on everyone a child meets and is a powerful argument for allowing abortion. I can understand the position of those who want to make abortion unavailable to the women using it as a method of birth control— having multiple abortions, never seeming to learn their lesson. It's a morbid way of doing things. However, rape is one instance in which an abortion is inarguably warranted, which means outlawing the practice under any and all circumstances would be inhumane. The act of being raped by one's male relative will lead to PTSD, in and of itself, but carrying the pregnancy to term could lead to insurmountable psychological difficulties for the mother. She may very likely commit suicide if she is not allowed to abort the baby. Anyone who withholds the right to lessen such a tragedy is expecting the mother to have coping skills that the vast majority of us do not have. This is an instance in which the woman needs to be seen for what she is—a victim of violence—and presented with treatment options.

I've seen rigid stances on medical treatments in my own extended family. Three relatives have been clinically diagnosed as needing medication for psychological issues. Two of them have attempted suicide and are, thus, a danger to themselves without that medication. Some family members, however, believe God made them that way on purpose and that the medication is not needed. The belief that mental health issues need not be treated the same as physical health issues still pervades many communities in our society, regardless of whether or not those communities are religious. Common sense tells us that whether the medical treatment a person needs is an abortion, an anti-depressant pill, or a round of chemotherapy, the patient's basic right to survival should trump all religious affiliation, and the treatment be given. Abortion and birth control can be just as important to survival as the anti-depressant or high blood pressure pills many of us take for granted.

Restricted or no access to birth control and abortion would not just be my problem, your problem, your girlfriend's problem, your sister's problem, etc. It would be everyone's problem. I don't care whether you support birth control because women do, because some men do, or because you believe God does; I just hope you support it. Because regardless of whether you support it and believe it's good for all of us, it is.

14 – THE "S" WORD

Sex is a dirty word for unmarried Christians. I lived a rather sheltered life directed by my parents' and grandparents' religious beliefs and didn't even learn about sex until science class in seventh grade. With the rise of the internet, I would imagine there is no way the kids born in recent years can be shielded from learning about it for that long.

Once I was deemed old enough to know what sex was, I was bombarded in church and the associated youth groups with messages about what constitutes sex (oral vs. petting vs. anal vs. vaginal) and what was allowed prior to marriage. Since the Baptist way of life is to take all religious teachings literally, I just assumed everything but vaginal penetration was allowed until you got married because that was how you kept your hymen intact and showed your husband you were pure on your wedding night. I assumed if I didn't bleed that night, I'd be rejected by him and cast out of my own family in shame once they found out. So, I started dating and set my limit at vaginal sex.

Through my teenage years with my first boyfriends, we did heavy petting and oral. I made it to college, and my first love and I engaged in anal sex. I chose that because I was too afraid of: 1) the shame of having "actual" sex before marriage, 2) the shame my family would feel if they found out I was taking birth control to have vaginal sex before marriage, and 3) getting pregnant, to try vaginal intercourse. So, throughout our relationship we did everything but.

Throughout my first real relationship and our sexual experimentation, I had horrible menstrual problems, including bleeding that lasted twenty-one days at its worst. I was at the gynecologist almost every week, trying to figure out what was wrong. My gynecologist refused to stick a speculum up in me to fully examine what was causing the bleeding because I told her I hadn't yet had vaginal sex. I will never forget the look on her face when she said, "Oh, sweetie... You haven't had sex?" I was twenty years old at the time, and I felt my face grow red with embarrassment and hot with anger— not at her, but at my church, parents, and grandparents. I have always regarded doctors as the keepers of knowledge about societal norms, because everyone goes to them. They have a feel for who is doing what and how many are doing the same things. It was clear to me that if I stuck out as an outlier to my own doctor, I was outside the norm. I felt betrayed by the two people who raised me to be afraid of an act that was, according to my doctor, entirely normal for people my age.

It took me no time to catch up... I basically walked out of the doctor's office that day and into bed with my then boyfriend. I was ready to join the ranks and get "it" over with. I didn't feel a rush of love or oxytocin that made me bond to him. I truly felt next to nothing on the emotional front. Regardless, I cried after our first time when I was alone in the shower with a multitude of things running through my head. First it was, "That's it? That wasn't even all that great.... Why do people go so crazy over this?" Then it was, "I've let God and my parents down... I didn't wait until I was married." It wasn't until a couple of boyfriends later, when I actually had fantastic sex, that I thought, "I'm glad I didn't stop with the first guy. I'm glad I didn't marry him... I could've had a sexually dissatisfying marriage and not even known what I was missing out on." Similarly, and sadly enough, I also felt very little physically the first time I had sex. After many more months of "doing it" with my boyfriend, it became clear to me that neither he, nor I, knew how to pleasure a woman and that penetration alone would not lead to my orgasm.

I can't say my experience is exactly the same as others raised in fundamentalist homes, but I do have friends whose experiences were similar. For example, a male friend of mine, who was raised as a devout Catholic and later turned atheist, informed me that his parents taught him premarital sex is a mortal sin. He spent his teenage years afraid a woman was going to have sex with him, which would lead to his death and eventual casting into hell. Yikes! I can't say that I also thought I would die if I had sex, but I did think my family would be ashamed of me and, perhaps, not love me anymore.

When I started to lose my faith, I googled most of the lessons I learned in church to see what the Bible ACTUALLY says about them. One of these lessons was that premarital sex is a sin. I think people's ability to search the Bible via the web is one of the reasons churches are rapidly losing followers in modern times. I wouldn't be surprised if the Bible was originally made to be as long as it is and always printed on the thinnest paper possible on purpose in order to deter people from actually reading it. When I was a kid (before the internet was invented), my family showed up at church every Sunday and simply trusted that what the pastor said was truly addressed somewhere in the Bible and must be heeded. Even in Bible studies, there was never any order to the passages that were read. We did not start at the beginning and make our way through the book in its entirety, because people would come and go and there was no possible way to keep everyone up to speed. I did notice, however, that certain passages were always homed in on, and others, even entire books in the Bible, were completely ignored. This shows how the book is often used as a weapon with specific passages selected and used to shame followers.

In my quest to learn what the Bible has to say about premarital sex, I stumbled upon *Deuteronomy 22:20-21*, which says *"But if the thing is true, that evidence of virginity was not found in the young woman, then they shall bring out the young woman to the door of her father's house, and the men of her city shall stone her to death with stones, because she has done an outrageous thing in Israel by whoring in her father's house. So you shall purge the evil from your midst."* This passage is filled with all sorts of crazy messages and blatant sexism. I was not around to validate whether this was where the infamous "double standard," by which men who sleep with many women are celebrated as studs and women who sleep with more than one man are shunned as whores, began. Nonetheless, I believe it might've been. Nowhere in this passage does it say that a man must be stoned to death if he is not a virgin when he marries, and I guarantee you it is no coincidence that the Bible was written entirely by men. No woman in her right mind would write and believe something so damaging to her self-esteem and potentially endanger her life. Further, no person who respects women, and people in general, would write such a thing. It's also no coincidence that African-Americans had nothing to do with the drafting of segregation laws. People do not write laws and rules that persecute themselves. Another obvious flaw in this passage is the requirement for evidence of virginity, which is believed to be an intact hymen. If people still took this passage literally today, women could be errantly stoned to death whose hymens broke while they were playing sports or inserting a tampon, well before they married. Ergo, to support the need for proof of virginity is to promote wrongful death in certain circumstances.

The mere presence of *Deuteronomy 22:20-21* in the Bible also proves the Christian god's love is not unconditional. Unconditional love does not involve death by stoning when a condition (i.e., staying chaste until marriage) is not met. With messages like these in their scriptures, it's no wonder Christians often suffer crippling anxiety. You would, too, if you thought someone could love you but still want you murdered. Christians claim their religion to be full of love, acceptance, and hope, but if you dig into their creed... it's full of judgment and death.

First Corinthians 7:8-9 also relates to premarital sex: *"To the unmarried and the widows I say that it is good for them to remain single as I am. But if they cannot exercise self-control, they should marry. For it is better to marry than to burn with passion."* If you combine this passage with *First Corinthians 7:1-5*, you see the Bible condones getting married to have a sex slave. Verses 7:1-5 read: *"Now concerning the matters about which you wrote: It is good for a man not to have sexual relations with a woman. But because of the temptation to sexual immorality, a man should have his own wife and each woman her own husband. The husband should give to his wife her conjugal rights, and likewise the wife to her husband. For the wife does not have authority over her own body, but the husband does. Likewise, the husband does not have authority over his body, but the wife does. Do not deprive one another, except perhaps by agreement for a limited time, that you may devote yourselves to prayer; but then come together again, so that Satan may not tempt you because of your lack of self-control."* Slaves were bought and commanded to serve their owners' desires, and brides were bought with a dowry to serve their husbands desires back in Biblical times. Do you see the similarity?

Other verses in the Bible talk about paying for sex. *Exodus 22:16* reads "*If a man seduces a virgin who is not betrothed and lies with her, he shall give the bride-price for her and make her his wife.*" I'm hoping you can see now how devout Christians came to be so fearful of sex. Some are afraid they will be stoned to death, others that they will be cast into hell, others that they will have to marry someone just because they slept with them, and women, especially, that their desires for love and sexual satisfaction don't matter at all. This verse from Exodus does not mention the woman's desire, or lack thereof, to marry the man in question.

Another overarching theme in the Bible is a lack of regard for fulfillment and happiness. If someone marries a person with whom they have no sexual chemistry, following the rules set forth in these Bible verses will make them miserable. They won't cheat because adultery is punishable by death or sentencing to hell, and they won't divorce to remove the temptation to cheat because their god hates divorce, according to *Malachi 2:16*. So, these people sentence themselves to a life of unhappiness in an unfulfilling marriage and convince themselves that life is not meant to be enjoyed.

Churchgoers often use the verses mentioned so far in this chapter to try to control women, yet they rarely mention the verses in *Ephesians* chapter five. *Ephesians 5:5* says *"For you may be sure of this, that everyone who is sexually immoral or impure, or who is covetous (that is, an idolater), has no inheritance in the kingdom of Christ and God."* Plenty of evidence exists to prove men have only limited control over their sexual desires (a.k.a. being covetous) regardless of whether they act on them, and this verse preaches that none of them will make it to heaven because of that. Unsurprisingly, Christian men rarely mention this verse to a woman because they would simultaneously have to acknowledge that it means they, too, are not going to heaven. I don't understand how people are missing this and why verses in Deuteronomy and First Corinthians are adhered to while those in Ephesians are entirely ignored. In my opinion, this further proves that the stories and rules in the Bible were simply made up by people attempting to judge and control others rather than by a loving, divine being.

Longevity is another important factor to consider when discussing views on premarital sex. The Bible was written back when people had much shorter lifespans and could marry multiple people. People could get married at age fifteen, which was roughly middle-aged back then. Having five wives and expecting them, in aggregate, to satisfy all the sexual urges of the remaining fifteen or so years of your life was feasible. These days, people can live more than one hundred years but only marry one person. Given the rise in the divorce rate, one could easily argue that expecting one person to satisfy all your sexual urges for a lifetime is not always sustainable.

After reading this chapter, I hope you can now see that looking to the Bible for advice on when and with whom to have sex, and of what type, is a shaky endeavor. Despite what the status quo in your religious community may be, you are better off establishing a status quon't that involves tuning in to your gut feelings and practicing safe sex rather than trying to be perfect and resisting all temptation.

15 – ONE SIZE DOESN'T FIT ALL

I believe in the power of meditation. I do not believe in the power of prayer. I believe in the healing power of a support group and attend support group meetings when I can. I don't believe I'm a bad person, or won't successfully heal, if I miss some of them.

Having recognized the inherent differences between all human beings, I don't believe there is a one-size-fits-all solution to our problems and unease. No book published past, present, or future has all the answers. Attendance of a certain type of weekly meeting will not universally help all people.

Most people recognize that we all have free will, but few of us can agree on why. I believe the very reason we have free will is to find our own, unique solutions to our problems. If there was one common solution which would work for all of us, we wouldn't need free will.

I will be forever grateful to the support group I attended, as one might say, "religiously," for one and a half years. It helped me make immense progress in healing the emotional wounds from my childhood. I had been in therapy for a few years prior, but the progress I made among others who could relate was much more rapid. After a year and a half, my progress plateaued, and I started reacting negatively to some things going on in the meeting rooms and with others I knew in the program, so my attendance became spotty.

During my childhood and teenage years, I was only in the good graces of my family and our church congregation if I went to church every Sunday and followed the rules in the Bible. The support group I went to also had large books and weekly meetings, and I began to get the exact same feelings of not being accepted when I skipped a few meetings or didn't read the book. Although this text was not full of crazy passages about stoning whores to death as is the Bible, I still didn't feel right making all my life decisions according to the guidance of a book. Not everyone in my group shunned me for pulling back, and I still keep in touch with those who didn't. But I did pull back from the people who judged me. One of the overarching lessons of support groups and therapy is that it's important to take care of yourself and make yourself comfortable. We can't all wear the same clothes and be comfortable, and we can't all practice the same recovery, spirituality, and religion and be comfortable – none of these is one size fits all.

When my progress peaked in my support group and I started to feel uncomfortable, I decided it was time to move on and seek out my own truth—outside of the group's text. I still pop into meetings occasionally and don't necessarily plan to stop going altogether because I still find them very helpful. I simply allow myself to go or not go, based on how I feel, rather than forcing myself to go to gain others' acceptance. The way I explained my now spotty attendance to a friend in my group was, "I don't want to go to the doctor when I'm not sick." Talking about problems every week at the meeting was starting to make me feel worse, not better, because I had worked through a lot of them already. So, I began to seek alternate schools of thought and new joyful experiences.

I find comfort in a lot of the Buddhist and Hindu mentalities, such as boundless awareness, collective consciousness, and nature's abundance. I do not, however, ascribe to a belief in reincarnation or a caste system. No one has been able to prove, with any reliable certainty, that in a past life they were something or someone else. I also don't believe that the situation we're born into should be our lot in life and never improve. Since a status quon't is not a complete rejection of the status quo, but rather, the utility of useful parts of it and the addition of new, I picked the beliefs and practices that healed and comforted me from Hindu, Buddhist and support group wisdom. This mashup has become my current, though ever-evolving, belief system. To me, knowing what I don't believe is as important as knowing what I do believe.

I do believe forgiving your parents for hurting you *can* be healing. I do not believe that forgiving one's parents for child abuse is *universally* healing. I also don't believe in prolonging relationships with people, be they relatives or not, if those relationships cause serious emotional distress. As such, I have not prolonged my relationships with one of my parents. I feel justified in taking this approach because I hold myself to the same standard. Had I abused or neglected someone for close to thirty years, I would in no way expect them to forgive me and keep our relationship going. In fact, I have hurt people in much less extreme ways and still not expected their forgiveness and a continued relationship.

I take the same approach to politics as I do to religion. It is nonsensical to me to identify as either "Democrat" or "Republican." Each political party has a certain, and often opposing, stance on various issues.

Having to identify as one or the other to run for office negates people's free will to have their own opinions and think critically. I do not identify with either political party because I support some views from each side. For example, I am pro-choice (a Democratic view), but I think Democrats sometimes overspend (a Republican view). I support free birth control (a Democratic view), and the list goes on. When I vote, I vote for the candidate that supports the belief(s) I find most important. I believed Obama supported women, LGBTQ rights, and education, so I voted for him in each election that he won. Women comprise roughly half of the US population, and a large portion of the male population is gay. Even though I thought Obama's presidency might lead to Democratic overspending, I decided I would rather this country go bankrupt than we elect a president who openly discriminates against over half the population. Mitt Romney was that discriminatory candidate, so the choice, for me, between him and Obama was clear. Unfortunately, the American people were faced with a similar choice in the 2016 presidential election—between someone who might overspend (Hillary Clinton) and someone who openly discriminates against more than half of the population (Donald Trump). The discriminatory side won this round, and the solutions he proposed are definitely not one size fits all.

I do not take all of a political candidate's views seriously. I understand that a large part of winning an election is having enough funding. In order to obtain such funding, a candidate must identify with one of the two big parties (Democratic or Republican) and endorse that party's views. This is the status quo, whereas I believe the status quon't should be allowing candidates to run with their own stances on the issues. A candidate could take what he or she likes from either party's views and leave the rest. If this happened, we might wind up with more palatable people in office and sustainable compromise among U.S. citizens. We can't stuff America into an extra-small blouse, with a garden variety politician, and be comfortable. We need a tailored solution.

16 – HOW YOU FEEL AT YOUR SPIRITUAL OR RELIGIOUS GATHERINGS

My family went to church every Sunday in our dress-up clothes and sat upright for hours on hard plastic chairs or in awkwardly constructed pews. The building was air-conditioned to, what felt like, near freezing. When it was time to worship, we stood for long periods of time, guessing at the notes because there were no hymnals and the songs were originals, written by the band. The entire experience was always uncomfortable for me. I hated the clothes I had to wear; I hated having to sit still and be quiet for several hours; and I hated being cold. I also didn't understand the point of dressing up when I had been told that God could see me at all times, so he knew what I looked like in my pajamas and even naked. When I got older, it became clear that we dressed up to earn the approval of others in the church.

Looking or acting a certain way to earn the approval of others does not feel good. The scowls from the Sunday School teacher when my hair was not neatly combed made me feel ashamed. The angry glares cast my way when I would fidget and make noise during the sermon made me feel embarrassed and unwanted. I was not allowed to run around and get dirty, make noise, and sleep in on Sundays. The environment was too rigid too soon. My discomfort aside, I also noticed that the adults in my family were not happy or comfortable in this environment. Since none of us was happy, free, and comfortable, I just assumed these feelings were not important in a religious setting.

At age thirty, I attended a gong lab, also called a sound bath, for the first time. I was comfortable and happy before, during, and after this spiritual gathering. The experience, in its entirety, was a stark contrast to the spiritual gatherings I had attended in Christian churches. In the gong lab, we all laid on the floor on mats, curled up with pillows and blankets. No dress code had been listed in the invite, and most showed up in sweatpants—none with their hair neatly styled or makeup perfectly done. It also didn't matter what anyone looked like because the room was darkened, and we were told to close our eyes. It was warm and cozy in there. One of the officiants burned sage to trigger our sense of smell and add to the sense of calm already permeating the room.

As the ceremony began, a woman spoke kind words in a soft voice and instructed all of us to relax, one body part at a time. After this guided meditation, instruments were played to drown out all external noise and tune us in to the rhythms of our bodies. I felt the drum beat in step with my heartbeat. I breathed along with the tempo. The woman then sang a beautiful song in words incomprehensible to those who only speak English. She did not ask anyone to sing along with her and, in fact, told us at the beginning of the ceremony that no participation would be required. All she asked of us was that we lay with our head towards the gong. I relaxed during the ceremony, feeling cared for and loved. All I had needed to do was make myself comfortable and enjoy.

The sound from the gong became so loud it drowned out any thoughts I had in my head. I understood that, unlike a sermon, which intends to fill the audience's brains with one specific thought, the point of the gong lab was to clear out all thoughts. The night ended with the singer speaking two poems softly into the microphone. The messages were positive; they were about not letting fear rule our lives and about fostering the love and kindness we all have inside of us. As I opened my eyes, though I had not fallen asleep, I felt drowsy and relaxed. I took my time sitting up. Having become so ensconced with the sound, I again noticed the smell of sage once it had been silenced, and I felt at peace.

Despite the guided meditation and spoken poems, I understood there was no singular, overarching lesson we were supposed to grasp; the takeaways from the experience would all be different— and that was okay. The takeaway could be nothing, and that was also okay. This was the opposite of my experience in church services, which were always geared towards a passage of the Bible. I took many wonderful ideas from the evening gong lab, but the most prominent was how it should feel when we practice our spirituality. I now understand that we should feel comfortable, relaxed, and loved in our practice. It's not worth the sacrifice of these three feelings to attend church every Sunday or practice any other religion that doesn't foster those feelings.

The gong lab had been a safe space for me to relax for an hour and a half. The lab does not take place every week. No routine attendance is required, nor even requested by anyone involved. Though if it had been, I would've gladly gone over and over again. I wanted to be there because I felt wonderful while I was there.

Hopefully, each of us can find such a place in this world and attend because we want to, not because we think God or our peers are taking attendance.

The instructors at the yoga studio in which I practice do not preach Hindu beliefs to their students. No one in the studio has ever asked me why I practice yoga, or whether a particular interest in Hinduism led me to the studio. Rather, they simply express their delight that I am there and wish to practice with them. The same goes for all students at the studio. It doesn't matter why we come together; it just matters that we do.

The students at my local yoga studio don't preach beliefs to get others to practice with them because they don't need to. The culture is one of attraction, not promotion. They are happy people, and others can sense that when they are around them. It is human nature to want to be happy, so when we see someone that has succeeded in becoming happy, we're likely to ask them what they do. My friends at the studio told me their happiness comes from practicing yoga frequently, meditating, and journaling. I tried these things in an effort to be happy myself, and I have mostly succeeded. I would love to live in a world where joy was the key driver in people's decisions, but at present, it is typically fear. Joy speaks for itself and would be easier to spread than fear. The Hindu practices of yoga and meditation attract people, rather than forcing their participation. If the religions, such as Catholicism or Baptism, that try to strong arm their followers into action had backed off the scare tactics and pursued joy, they might have attracted larger, warmer communities than they could have ever imagined. Forcing people to be together makes them fall apart, whereas allowing them to be attracted to each other in a comfortable setting makes them fall together.

17 – GASLIGHTING STARTED B.C.

Gaslighting is a form of emotional abuse in which true information is twisted or selectively omitted to favor the abuser. It can also be the introduction of false information in order to make the victim doubt his or her own perceptions—and even sanity. People often date this practice back to 1938 when the play *Gas Light* was written. In the play, a man dims the lights in his house and denies the lower level of illumination when his wife mentions it to him. He makes her doubt what she is truly seeing. Although it did not yet have a catchy name, this practice existed long before the play was written, even before Christ allegedly arrived on earth.

We all know that messages received from God, or any other divine being, are never received in a provable format. No one hears a booming voice from the sky answering their prayers; if they had, the video would have gone viral by now. Likewise, God does not send emails that can be forwarded on to others, and so on. Therefore, the use of his teachings is entirely up to an interpretation of hearsay. With the rise of satirical newspapers, such as *The Onion*, it's also surprising to me that people believe everything in the Bible is absolute truth simply because it was written down. I can see from the sexist and homophobic tilt of the Bible that straight men in Biblical times were already using a gaslighting strategy for their own agendas.

Imagine yourself a woman of small stature alive in biblical times, asking why you aren't allowed to speak in church. A male contemporary tells you the reason why is that God—someone you have never heard from—said so. You might slough this man off as a jerk who is lying to you, but if all the disciples or a church congregation sided with him, leaving you the odd one out, you might start to doubt your feelings. Outnumbered and surrounded by men twice your size, you would also likely realize that, for your personal safety's sake, you don't have the option to disagree. In this particular time period, people had limited methods to verify hearsay. You were not with this man when he allegedly heard from God, so his story is hearsay and most likely corroborated by his friends who claim to have been there and heard it, too. We've all heard stories of men covering for one of their boys, telling his wife or girlfriend he was with them the whole night when he mysteriously stopped responding to her text messages. I would argue the same thing happened in Biblical times.

In 2017, if someone walked into a room full of people saying, "A snake told me to eat an apple from a tree," or "A burning bush told me to move a large group of people out of Egypt," everyone would 1) laugh, and 2) ask for proof. Burning bushes do not talk—or someone near a California wildfire would have caught a message from the divine on his or her cellphone by now. Similarly, no one has ever recorded a snake talking in the history of time, let alone speaking a language a human could understand. If I had to guess what actually happened, it's that Adam told Eve a snake wanted her to eat an apple, and although she didn't believe him, she obliged because she was afraid he would hurt her if she didn't. Regardless of whether the story of Adam and Eve ever happened, I hope I've successfully illustrated that the story could have been made up and used for emotional manipulation.

Parallels can also be drawn to homosexuality. Homosexuality is accepted by many more people today than it has ever been, as evidenced by the Supreme Court of the United States allowing same sex marriage as of June 26, 2015. However, it is still less common than heterosexuality. Therefore, homosexual people still face some of the same dangers of being outnumbered. The straight men who wrote the Bible claimed that a divine being outlawed homosexuality as an abomination. They also tried to manipulate anyone practicing such sexuality into believing that it was wrong. If such sexuality felt wrong to these people, they would not practice it, but it actually feels natural to them. By claiming it is wrong, these heterosexual men made homosexuals doubt their own feelings and perceptions, and it's a shame. A lot of pain has been caused by the gaslighting technique.

Another example of gaslighting is the story of Jesus walking on water, which was used to convince people he was divine. Eyeglasses had not yet been invented when this allegedly happened, so such a stunt would be easy to pull off. Perhaps the people who think they saw him walk on water were so far away they couldn't see the rocks just beneath the surface of the water that he was actually standing on. We all know that cutting someone in half would lead to their demise, yet we can all believe we've seen such an event at a magic show. It's a matter of altering perceptions of reality. In contrast to Biblical stories, magic shows are an invitation to have one's perceptions distorted. The audience elects, and even consciously pays for tickets, to attend the show, so this does not constitute gaslighting.

Gaslighting leads to intense anger and distress in its victims. I've been gaslighted many times in my life and felt these feelings myself. The reaction of anger and distress is appropriate because it is a reaction to mistreatment. Many articles have been written in recent years on men's use of gaslighting in romantic relationships in order to manipulate women. Such articles have had the positive effect of raising awareness in interpersonal relationships, but it's another thing entirely to recognize it in your religion. Therefore, I believe this recognition to be the next wave of feminism.

Any Christian feminists who have been questioning whether some things they learn in church actually happened need to consider that their pastors, priests, etc. may be gaslighting them. Part of the definition of gaslighting is that it benefits the abuser, and we all know it is to men's benefit to keep women oppressed, a practice the Christian church undoubtedly supports. Men benefit most if women are not allowed control over their own reproductive systems. It helps keep men's competition out of the workforce and financially dependent on them. Men benefit most if equal pay is not given to women. Men benefit if they convince a woman she cannot sleep with someone until she marries him because many women would not willingly marry a man if they knew he was ill-endowed or over-endowed, depending on her own anatomy, or horrible in bed. Men benefit by convincing women they must submit to their husbands. Men benefit when they convince a woman that she is to blame for his lust and that she can control it by looking a certain way. The examples are numerous, but all absolve men of any responsibility for their actions and dismiss women's reactions as unmerited.

Do you see the pattern yet? The entire invention of religion was an exercise in the introduction of false information to manipulate others to the benefit of abusers — the exact definition of gaslighting. Anyone who has their rights trampled on automatically questions why it was done. Biblical men trampled on women's and homosexuals' rights and convinced them that their perceptions of being hurt were unfounded. Those women and homosexuals had a right to feel outraged, and modern-day feminists are outraged for them.

I don't blame women or homosexuals for going along with Biblical teachings in the past, but today people have more options. If we receive false information, we can demand that someone prove their claims (e.g., "show me the email/video/text"). We are no longer outnumbered and helpless. We have police to respond to domestic violence claims. We have shelters for women. We have witness protection programs, and the list goes on. What we don't have enough of, however, are people who have the courage to question the false information they've been given in church. We need to tell church leaders that we quon't accept their claims without proof. We need to trust our perceptions if the teachings of the church make us feel sick because that's our bodily perception of being lied to. You don't need a man, a church, or a text to validate your perceptions: the proof is in your gut. You just need to find the courage to trust yourself.

18 – THE CONDITIONS OF HIS UNCONDITIONAL LOVE

We all learn the concept of unconditional love at some point in our lives, but many of us have never actually experienced it. Love does not come easily from the Christian god, so, in turn, love did not come easily to me in my devout Christian family. In order to receive love, I was expected to look my best, never swear, always share, rarely cry, pray all the time, and, in general, always obey what my parents and grandparents told me to do. If I did all these things, sometimes I got praise and or a hug. Even when I earned scraps of love, I still felt ripped off. Being praised for what you've done (i.e., meeting all the conditions) will never be as fulfilling as being praised for who you are (i.e., unconditionally).

It's impossible to feel appreciated when you had to beg someone to love you and stay with you. Having to earn love sets a person up on a shaky ground of rampant insecurity; he'll be afraid that if he changes or forgets what he did to receive that love, it will go away. In my case, I was so exhausted from all the work it took to get my parents' and grandparents' (and God's, for that matter) approval that, often, by the time I got it I didn't want it anymore. I also couldn't celebrate and relish the praise because I knew I wouldn't have it for long. I always had to do something even better to get another dose. I didn't feel loved for who I was because I was only in good graces when I was who they wanted me to be.

I tried to follow the teachings of the Bible for way too many years in hopes that God would love me and treat me well. As I pulled away from my religion, I was also afraid he would punish me with illness, job loss, or some other tragedy that would decrease my quality of life. Oddly enough, the opposite has happened. I found a job with flexible hours that allowed time for me to pursue my creative endeavors. I've grown closer to extended family members who love me for who I am and with whom I enjoy spending time. I have better friends who are more capable of two-way relationships than my old friends were, etc.

Once I stopped trying to earn love, love found me. I like the teachings of Deepak Chopra for this reason. He teaches of the universe's endless abundance of positive energy and love which should come easily to you if you flow with the energy of the universe. In many of his daily guided meditations, he strongly advises against struggling to get what you want. Instead, he encourages us to believe we deserve to be happy and fulfilled and let good things come to us. From personal experience, I know how much better it feels to be loved when I wasn't trying to make the person love me. I'm able to celebrate that love and praise because I'm not worried I'll lose it. I know that it came to me when I was being my authentic self, and that I don't have to do anything in particular or be someone else to continue to receive it. This love came instantly from friends I've made in recent years and from the extended family members to whom I've grown closer. I now believe in unconditional love, but I had to pull away from my religion, which claimed to teach it, in order to receive it.

I'd encourage anyone who is trying to make someone love them to stop. I can guarantee that if you stop trying to earn love and instead focus on being your authentic self, real love will come to you. It may not be from the person that you think you want it from, but once you experience real, effortless love from someone else, you'll likely decide you wouldn't have been satisfied with the kind of love that particular person would have offered. You'll start to see how unfulfilling it would be, and it will become undesirable. Similarly, if you stop trying to make a deity love you, and you let the people here on earth love you, you may want God's love less, just as I do. You'll want real love you can feel, regardless of where it comes from. Besides, how could you expect to keep God's love when you would have to follow an 800,000-word rule book to do so? Please don't put your hopes of feeling real, unconditional love on the shelf until you die in hopes of receiving that love in heaven; you'll miss too many opportunities to feel it here.

19 – RANDOM EFFECTS WITH NO SENSIBLE CAUSE

Some effects in life have definite causes, and others are entirely random. For example, if you swing and hit a ball with a bat, the ball will move. The swing is the cause, and the movement of the ball is the effect. In contrast, your car being struck by lightning while driving through a storm is entirely random; there is no cause. Any other car on the same road could have been struck, and there is no particular reason it was yours. Humanity is more comfortable with cause and effect than it is with randomness, so a key function of religion has been to explain random events as cause and effect. A religious friend may explain that lightning struck your car because you haven't been "saved" and God is angry with you. By inventing religion, humans attempted to turn the unknowable and unpredictable into the predictable and preventable. Failing to find causes for certain effects within the natural realm on earth, they then pointed to the supernatural realm. When this approach provides comfort, it can be a good thing, but when it causes us to point fingers at our fellow man, it can simply be cruel.

When something horrible happens to someone we love, many of us look back on the events leading up to the tragedy in hopes of explaining why it happened to them and not us. We compare events of their life to our own and reassure ourselves that "it could never happen to me." For example, let's say your good friend gets lung cancer at age forty-six. You may look back at his life and remember that he smoked cigarettes every day from ages fifteen to thirty-five and assume he got lung cancer from the smoking. You then remember that you smoked every day, but only for two years, and convince yourself that because you smoked substantially fewer cigarettes, you'll never get lung cancer. This practice of reflection and comparison fails us when there were no events prior to the cancer that would have logically led to the outcome. If our friend had never smoked a cigarette and was a marathon runner, then it would seem as if lung cancer could randomly strike anyone—even us. Getting scared, we will lean on our god, if we believe in one.

"God's plan" is a phrase that has been used by people for decades upon decades to explain the inexplicable. These words are often uttered in hopes of giving comfort to someone who cannot make sense of a tragedy that just happened, but they usually just make that person angry at God and the person who spoke them. For example, consider a parent—we'll call him John—whose young child is struck by lightning during his soccer game and dies. His friend Jason's first response is, of course, "I'm so sorry for your loss." Behind the scenes, though, Jason may begin to judge John for not heeding a warning from the weather man, not taking his son out of the game early, or any number of reasons he can think of to point to how the outcome is John's fault. Jason doesn't do this because he thinks, or wants to think, that his friend is a bad person. Rather, Jason does this to comfort himself with the belief that he has control over whether something similar could happen to his own son. However, in this story Jason's son was playing in the same soccer game but was not struck by lightning. Jason also had no warning that a severe thunderstorm would so rapidly approach, and he cannot come up with a logical reason why such an awful thing has happened to his friend John and his son. Failing to find a cause for the effect, Jason offers the words,

"Everything happens for a reason; I'm sure it's part of God's plan" to John.

In this story, Jason has only comforted himself. By not acknowledging the event as random, he doesn't deal with his fear that he or his son could suffer a similar fate to John's son. Meanwhile, he has upset his friend John. John feels as though Jason has minimized his loss by implying that it's not a real tragedy because it was supposed to happen. A more compassionate approach would be to assure John that the event was entirely random, there was nothing he could have done to prevent it, and his feelings of devastation are entirely justified. Even if John believed that what Jason told him was true, it still wouldn't make him feel better. He may become jealous of Jason, wondering why God's plan involved his own son's demise, rather than Jason's.

When people attempt to explain the inexplicable, they blame people for things they have no control over, layering guilt on top of grief. The world would be a much more inviting place to live in if we didn't attempt to do this. It is just as stressful to live a life in which you believe you are responsible for everything that happens to you as it is to live a life you feel you have no control over. There needs to be a balance between the two — affect what you can and acknowledge the rest as unsolved mysteries. Teetering to either extreme leads to a narrow existence or reckless endangerment, neither being the superior choice. But regardless of what our friends will say about our life choices, we all need to decide what we'll tell ourselves about them. If we take chances and bad things happen, will we beat ourselves down with relentless guilt? If we take chances and good things happen, will we chalk it up as dumb luck?

I am currently in my thirties and have three living grandparents, all in their mid-to-late eighties. Given my genes, I have the potential for great longevity. I could easily live another fifty-plus years. However, in my eyes, I have already lived a full life. If I die young, I would not view that as a tragedy because I feel the full truth of the saying "It's not the years in your life, it's the life in your years that matters." I have traveled, made friends, fallen in love, made love, been drunk, stayed up late, laughed until I cried, broken rules, eaten delicious food, sung at the top of my lungs, danced in the desert, grieved losses, and a number of other experiences that I find synonymous with a full life. It would be a tragedy to be afraid to try things for fear of being responsible for the brevity of one's life. I have to try new things in order to have a full life, regardless of how long it is. I believe this is why we all need to develop a level of comfort with the inexplicable, too: it will enrich our lives. Rather than spending months or years lamenting bad things that happened to me and trying to figure out how to prevent them in the future, I need to simply accept that they happened. Whether I caused them or they were entirely random does not change the fact that they happened, nor does it change what my options are in the present. It also does not change the fact that other things, preventable or random, will happen to me in the future.

New studies are published, seemingly every few months, on causes of cancer. For a while, the news focused on a study that proved drinking out of plastic water bottles with BPA in them could cause cancer. One study was published showing birth control prevents ovarian cancer and breast cancer but may cause cervical cancer. The latest study I've seen says eating bacon and processed meats causes colon cancer. In summary, there is probably a study published about any action, food, or drink that a person could possibly do or consume, linking each to some type of cancer. There are also people in the world who try to avoid all the things mentioned in these studies and still get cancer. We have a choice to be constantly in fear, avoiding all the things that could end our life, or to take moderate risks and let the chips fall where they may. In my opinion, it's much healthier to accept the uncertainty of how we will die and do the things that leave us fulfilled. We cannot predict everything that will happen to us, and not everything that happens to us happens for a reason. A more productive question than "why did this happen?" is "what do I want to do now?"

20 – THE ORIGINAL DRESS CODE

The story of Adam and Eve in the Garden of Eden involves a talking snake tempting Eve to eat an apple and then her tempting Adam to partake of the fruit. Let's set aside the absurdity of the fact that throngs of people believe: a) this actually happened, and b) this has any significance for all people. The key point of the story, for the purposes of this chapter, is that it was used to blame Eve for something that Adam, who was an adult male, did of his own free will. She can present an airtight case full of reasons he should eat the apple, but, at the end of the day, it's still his choice whether or not to eat it. In the scriptures, he should've been held equally responsible for his choices, but instead he got to blame Eve. Thus, the culture of blaming women for controlling (or failing to control) grown men's thoughts and choices began.

Many years A.D., dress codes were created to blame women for men's sexual thoughts and choices. The original dress code began in the Garden of Eden, according to the book of *Genesis* in the Bible, which describes Adam and Eve sewing fig leaves together to cover their loins after having eaten the forbidden fruit. I was raised in an extremely conservative church that enforced all sorts of rules governing what women were allowed to wear, but their rules paled in comparison to Muslim requirements. The overarching message from either religion is "cover up as much of yourself as you can at all times, so as not to tempt men to lust after you." Before my age reached double digits, I remember hearing these kinds of messages and following these kinds of rules. I wish I could say only women "of a certain age" have to deal with these kinds of restrictions, but there are plenty of perverts in the world who lust after children. The pervasive victim-blaming culture is truly sick, and it starts far too young.

Corporate America is another institution that has typically enforced strict dress codes. At one of my first corporate jobs, a male friend of mine informed me that a group of male coworkers sat in a conference room one afternoon discussing the curvature of my ass and how fantastic it looks in a pair of pants. None of these men had asked me to wear anything different or spoken a word about their attraction to me. Yet later that same year, my female boss pulled me aside saying a senior consultant had complained that a skirt of mine was too short and asked her to tell me to wear different things. I was LIVID. I'm sure the response she was expecting was, "I understand. I'll wear longer skirts and buy some new outfits." Equipped with the knowledge of the conversation about my ass, I seethed, "I've been told I'm equally distracting in pants; the problem is not what I wear. Tell him if he has trouble controlling sexual thoughts and urges, then he can work from home and find a support group." The problem with this situation in my workplace, which I know many other women have encountered, is that a male tried to make me responsible for controlling his thoughts. Luckily, I realized this as an impossible endeavor and refused to even try.

Any woman who has been catcalled or flirted with when she is in no way trying to attract a man's attention knows that she cannot control the lust of another person. I have personally thwarted sexual advances from men when I put no effort into my appearance—baggy sweatpants, no makeup, hair pulled back in a messy ponytail, sweaty from a workout, etc. The fact that women are lusted after when they are as ugly as they can possibly be proves my point.

In fact, men still have sexual urges even when women are physically removed. Clergymen in the Catholic church have been convicted of child molestation. Rape happens in all-male prisons. Stories are not published blaming the children or male prisoners for what they were wearing when the abuse happened, so why are women blamed? Blaming any victim for unwanted sexual advances is absurd, regardless of the victim's gender or age.

People would scoff if an alcoholic requested that every bar in America be shut down because their presence was making drinking alcohol too tempting. Instead, Alcoholics Anonymous was started for alcoholics to gain support and hold each other accountable for their consumption. Similarly, if a racist requested that all non-Caucasian people leave his town so he would not be tempted to make racist comments, people would not oblige. Asking all women to hide their skin and bodies to prevent rape and sexist comments is more of the same, but it's a practice that has been promoted for centuries. It is unfair—and impossible—to try to change the environment to prevent all types of acting out. The urge to act out, rather than the intended victims, is what needs to be addressed.

Requiring women to change their appearances also does not successfully remove discomfort; it merely transfers it from men to women. For example, in the past

I've obliged requests to change into lower heels to make male coworkers, friends, and boyfriends more comfortable with how tall I am, but their discomfort and insecurity was then transferred to me. Ignorance truly was bliss, but their words made me aware of someone watching me and disapproving of me. My ignorance prior to the requests proves I wasn't trying to provoke these jealous, judgmental, or lustful glances, but by suggesting my choice of shoes was incorrect, they were blaming me for having caused them. Ladies, we are not to blame for any male discomfort with our appearance. By creating and enforcing dress codes, society has put responsibility for preventing harassment and rape on the wrong shoulders. It's time for women to put it back where it belongs.

For as long as I can remember, it has also been the status quo to expect women to be physically appealing at all times. We are expected to increase a man's physical urges and sexual attraction to us while simultaneously decreasing both to an acceptable level. It's an impossible task that is not worth pursuing.

Like most women, I am not able to look physically appealing at all times, and the expectation that I try has caused me much suffering over the years. I've been told I'm ugly in the morning, I look bad with my hair pulled back, I need hair extensions, I should lose weight, I should gain weight, I should wear more makeup, I should wear less makeup, and on and on. The overall message has been "you are unattractive in your natural state, so change or hide what you can." Puberty was especially hard, but I outgrew my acne and got my braces off, eventually. Even though I looked more conventionally attractive, I still carried the scars from being constantly bullied about my appearance. I suffer from the infamous "ugly duckling" syndrome, and it breaks my heart that I don't see a pretty girl in the mirror staring back at me.

I've had many sleepless nights because of the traumas I've suffered in relation to my looks. Countless women share my pain, worrying about aging because a lot of men will value them less as their looks fade. Society's obsession with beauty is causing all of us pain, even the most physically attractive among us, because one can only be beautiful so many hours of the day and for so many years. Some cannot be conventionally, physically beautiful at all. Eventually, hair starts growing out of men's ears, everyone's faces get wrinkly, women's boobs sag, etc. Moments of being considered beautiful are fleeting, at best, and measuring our value in terms of anything that isn't timeless is unhealthy.

Luckily, I don't get criticized for much beyond my looks because I'm talented, smart, and successful, but it's pitiful to me that society still values my physical beauty (or lack thereof) above any of those traits, simply because

I'm female. If I were a man, comments about my unattractiveness would likely hurt me less (or potentially never be uttered) because my other traits would likely be pointed out to me more often and held in greater esteem.

A lot of men don't realize how much anxiety they get to avoid simply by being male. Society does not expect men to look good all the time. In fact, a large portion of society doesn't expect men to be physically attractive at all. Meanwhile, women's razor commercials show a person shaving an already hairless leg. Advertisers won't even show women in their natural state while trying to sell them something to "improve" on that state. I have been on dates with men who told me, "Women have it easy. They just look cute and then we do all the work." I proceeded to tell both that they don't realize how much effort it takes to look "cute" all the time. I realize expectations have long been placed on men to make a lot of money and be successful, but women have already eased up on these. Studies show that women are earning more degrees than men and account for over half the workforce these days. So, now women don't expect men to look good OR make money, but they expect THEMSELVES to look good all the time AND make money. Women have added more to our plates by removing it from men's. We now need men to lighten our load by easing up on their expectations of physical perfection.

I've also never liked the concept of "best self" or "worst self." In my opinion, rather than trying to be better than others or even better than our former selves, we should try to be our "truest" selves. It is not necessarily better or worse to be fatter or skinnier, shorter or taller, more toned or squishier than you are now. Striving to be one way or the other, rather than embracing who we are in the present moment, has made our culture sick and tired.

Thanks to the internet and the rise of social media, women all over the world are already showing that they quon't accept the current state of affairs. Dove, Always, and even regular moms whose posts have gone viral have started body positivity campaigns. These campaigns are great, and I think walks, similar to the Susan G. Komen walk for breast cancer, should be held to raise awareness of their cause. If a walk to raise awareness for body positivity was held in a large city, flyers with the YouTube web address for the Always "Like a Girl" commercials could be passed out to attendees. Rather than finding friends to donate to the cause, walkers could fund their own participation and wear shirts that say, "I am my biggest supporter" to fit with the theme. Everyone needs to know how much pressure girls feel to be conventionally attractive, as well as just how young they are when that pressure starts. These walks would promote that awareness. The statistics I have seen about the percentage of women who actually believe they are beautiful are heartrendingly low, and I think these statistics could spark shock and change if the information was widely distributed, particularly at an event that draws a crowd.

Men need to be involved in the body positivity movement, too. This is not only to deal with their own bodily insecurities, but also to introduce women to the men who will actually love them for who they are, not how they look. For me, personally, it's easy enough to be around women because I know they will love me and want to be around me even if I am unattractive. However, I struggle with a belief that most men are shallow and will not afford me the same love, regardless of my physical attractiveness. After all, a man who embodies such a view was just elected president of the United States. I know I'm not alone in my belief that if I start loving myself regardless of how I look, it doesn't necessarily mean all men will do the same. However, a body positivity awareness walk could be a place for women to meet the men who will.

Several body positive campaigns are trying to make the concept that "everyone is beautiful just as they are" catch on. I think a healthier concept would be "not everyone needs to be beautiful, so be as you are." Personally, I am exhausted from trying to be beautiful all the time because it's not what I naturally am. I have the ability to look physically attractive when I try, but I can look very unattractive with no makeup on and greasy hair pulled back into a ponytail. Numerous women share my same anxieties about someone catching them in their natural state. The hashtag "wokeuplikethis" made everything worse because It only celebrates women who society finds naturally attractive. I also don't understand why natural beauty is so much more valued than manufactured beauty. Inherited fortunes are not as attractive to most of us as the story of a self-made woman who worked for every dollar she has, so why is the reverse true when it comes to her appearance? A face with makeup can be just as pleasing to look at as a naturally beautiful face, in the same way the purchasing power of inherited dollars equals that of dollars earned through hard work.

Although I often worry about men's opinion of my attractiveness, I know that I, like many women, am holding myself back from true happiness. The keynote speaker at a conference I attended two years ago unintentionally revealed herself as sharing my same fear. Prior to starting her speech, she derailed her planned remarks to comment on how the emcee had offended her by implying how old she was. After her speech, the emcee returned to the stage to facilitate the Q&A session, and before he could get started, she forced him to say that she's "still got it", meaning her looks hadn't faded despite her increasing age. I was appalled. The woman could not have had more credentials, experience, and achievements to be proud of, yet here she was, in front of a crowd, focusing on her age and, what she perceived to be, her declining looks. Her resume was much more decorated than the emcee's, and by conventional standards, she was much more attractive than he. Yet, she wanted his approval. As women, we put our power in men's hands and ask them for validation that we should be giving ourselves because society tells us to. This woman tied her worth to her age and how she looks, as opposed to who she is. I reacted strongly to this scene, not because I was judging the woman, but because I identified with that feeling. I became painfully aware of the need to change my own attitude because I now saw how long such a debilitating belief can persist. That woman may go on believing she is worth less and less with each passing year, each new wrinkle, and each gray hair, and it breaks my heart. Although this woman is holding herself back, she also faces women who hold each other back.

The patriarchy may have started the whole mentality of judging a woman based on her looks, but women bought into it somewhere along the line and began competing with each other for men's attention. One strategy was to try to be prettier than every girl you knew. Girls adopting this approach would spend hours at the gym, swear off all carbohydrates, drink nothing but water, and so on. They also would surround themselves only with girls considered less attractive than they are. Another strategy, for those who might not be able to be the prettiest one, was to make prettier girls believe they weren't actually pretty. Thus, a mental war was waged on conventionally attractive women—picking at the tiniest of their flaws as if they are the only things people see when they look at them. An insecure woman is less likely to go after your man because you've made her think she doesn't deserve him. So, women have been at war with themselves and with each other for decades, but the media has waged a particularly vicious war on them as well.

Beauty is entirely subjective, but once the media creates an image to strive for, people start objectively picking apart anyone who doesn't look like the image. Billions upon billions of dollars have been made from this strategy by constantly changing the image. Thigh gaps became an overnight obsession. Thighbrows were lauded less than a year later. Thin eyebrows were in twenty years ago, and now thick brows are the trend. Thousands of women who removed eyebrow hair that won't grow back are feeling insecure because now they don't have the thick brows that are presently considered beautiful. Some are even resorting to microblading, which is basically a temporary tattoo, to replace the eyebrow hairs that won't grow back. Everyone is constantly striving for an image that they'll never be able to reach because it will change by the time they get there.

We've made ourselves poor. Most women have spent more than they care to admit on beauty products, diet pills, and/or gym memberships. Even those who don't spend much money on outer beauty products but flip through magazines wishing they looked like the women in photo-shopped images are spiritually poor. It's not natural for all of us to look the same, and we're crushing our spirits while trying. We're all scared, too. Many women are scared that if they stop buying beauty products and begin valuing themselves for who they are, then a man won't want to date them, and they'll no longer fit in with their female friends. Until the majority of women cease seeing each other as competition and men stop valuing only the most attractive females, the step away from beauty obsession is not going to happen. We need to create a soft place to land and a sense of community when we take that step, because most of us are more afraid of being alone than of being ugly. We only fear being ugly because the media tells us that is what leads to being alone. Sadly, the media's standards have been raised so high lately that most people view "imperfect" as synonymous with "ugly". So, even some of the most conventionally attractive women among us don't feel beautiful or good enough.

I have never liked the phrase "physical imperfection." To call something an imperfection is to assert that there is a universal standard for what is perfect, but matters of physical attraction are so subjective that such a standard could not possibly exist. For example, my two best friends in high school and I all had different "types" of guys we were into. I liked tall and muscular, Melissa liked an average height and build, and Julie liked short and skinny. Julie's penchant for shorter guys was not a quest to embrace "short" as an imperfection. She perceived that body type as perfect, mainly because she is also short. Similarly, I perceived tall guys as perfect, mainly because I am tall. There is no universal height that all women agree is perfect. Therapists often condone the use of "I" statements, such as "I feel" or "I think" to acknowledge the subjective ways in which we all perceive the world. I believe the world would be a much happier place if the status quo was to say, "I find you attractive" rather than, "you are attractive." This would take beauty from being something we have or don't have to being something we all have depending on who is looking at us. It would be ever present in all of us.

The quest to always be attractive also ignores the limitations of our bodies due to genetics. After a certain point, it's physically impossible for some people to gain weight and for others to lose it. The person who cannot lose weight might not be aware of their inability to lose it until after they've already put weight on. Shaming them for this lack of knowledge, as well as for the weight gain, helps no one. There's also no guarantee that once they lose it, they'll like their appearance better. I've met moms who had surgery to remove excess skin, post-pregnancy, and seen articles on the internet about men who have lost massive amounts of weight but are not happy with their skin folds, either. In my opinion, people look their best when they're happy, and we're not all happy at the same size. For instance, I think I might like my appearance more if I lost twenty pounds, but I know I would be less happy because I would have to give up some of the delicious food I eat. Replacing a happy smile with thinner thighs is not worth it to me. I'm happy at my current size even if it's not what another person considers "skinny" or "perfect." I did not come to be happy at my current size overnight, though; it required a journey.

I've been on a purposeful journey of trying to emotionally evolve for about five years now. Several of my friends have said "you seem better." I don't see myself as "better" now than I was five years ago, but rather, "more me" than I was. Sure, I was much more depressed, stressed, and physically unhealthy five years ago, but that's not because I was my "worst" self back then. I wasn't even a "self" at that time: the person I was, was not me. I was whoever everyone else wanted me to be, and I know I'm not the only one who grew up like that. I had been trying to please others for as long as I could remember, and it ultimately resulted in me not being someone most people wanted to be around. I had to focus on being someone *I* wanted to be around, rather than guessing at who *others* wanted to be around. On this journey, I learned that whenever I try to cover up who I am to please someone else, I become physically ill. I get strep throat or a cold sore, feel nauseous, lose sleep, etc. I now believe our bodies and our souls are so desperate to be authentic that they physically make us ill when we ignore those pleas.

For a brief period of time, I wanted to be a yoga instructor. I had planned my opening remarks to my first class to be, "Do whatever is the *most* you during the exercises. Whether you're a go-getter and want to do thirty-five one legged pushups or someone who wants to relax and do seven of them on your knees, it does not matter." A go-getter does not need to relax any more than a relaxed person needs to push themselves. Each needs to be exactly who they are, which will change from day to day, and they should allow their actions to ebb and flow accordingly. In true Capricorn fashion, I am a go-getter and a perfectionist. I had other planned opening remarks for a yoga class about New Year's resolutions and how they should be personal. Unlike most people, my resolutions are typically to "do less" because I struggle with knowing when to let up. This is not to say that for me to relax more is better than for me to push myself, but rather, it's an acknowledgement that my true self is not an overachiever. The real me likes balance. For example, I used to work out every single day even if I was sick and exhausted (which was most of the time, because of this habit) and work until very late at night. In the past few years, I've discovered that I prefer to work out a few times a week and do enough work to progress through the ranks at a measured, not accelerated, pace. I value free time and sleep more than additional dollars in my bank account. I had to challenge the corporate status quo (climbing the ladder as fast as you can in order to increase your salary as much as you can) to find a balanced lifestyle that makes ME happy, not one that is "better" than another's or "perfect."

Another part of living a balanced life is my pursuit of a romantic partner with balanced expectations. I don't want a partner who lies to me and tells me I look attractive 100% of the time when I know it's not true. I'm willing to bet most women out there don't actually want that either. We want our significant other to care less about how we look. It also bugs me when people talk about how skinny I am because I know that I'm not. I haven't been super skinny since the ninth grade, which is when I was still recovering from an eating disorder. I'm obviously healthier now but also comfortable with not being what society views as "skinny." I would rather people accurately describe me as fit or athletic, or say nothing at all about my build. I want people to tell me I'm more than my looks—that they love me for who I am. The truth is that my worth is not tied to my looks, nor is anyone else's.

Many of us, including myself, often act like we're bringing a fatal flaw to a relationship when we appear less than conventionally attractive. We act as if we can't make our partner laugh without our mascara on or our hair combed, as if it's our hair and eyelashes that tell our jokes. We act as if we can't hold our partner and comfort him if our arms are chubby. No matter the example, the subtext is feeling as though our appearance is what creates the distance in a relationship. Societal messaging affirms that feeling, piling on celebrities who "let themselves go" to blame them for their marriages and relationships falling apart. But in magazine-speak, to "let herself go" means she gained all of five pounds, or he didn't shave his face for a week. A vacation beard doesn't blow up a healthy, fulfilling relationship any more than five pounds of holiday weight does; an inability to be kind and available is what creates distance in a relationship. Many of us stop combing our hair in the first place because our partner is rarely around, or we start seeking comfort in food *because* our partner is unkind or physically unavailable to otherwise comfort us. None of us truly *needs* a pretty person to look at. If looks could fulfill our needs, we would be satisfied with pictures on our phones, but we're not. What we all truly need is arms around us, eye contact, a voice on the phone, facetime... and not just one of these things, *all* of them. We need someone who consistently shows up in a coherent, emotionally available state.

Now, I know some of you—okay, many of you— are thinking to yourselves, "But why are you saying people can become obese and blame their partners?" or "How hard is it to brush your hair?" Rest assured, I am not encouraging laziness, a lack of hygiene, or obesity. I am pointing out that people who feel fulfilled in relationships take care of their hygiene and watch their weight, because they already feel good and want that feeling to continue. There is equal responsibility for each person in a relationship to ensure his or her needs are being met and to leave said relationship if those needs cannot consistently be met. In other words, if you feel like you have to eat a lot in order to comfort yourself, you are responsible for asking your partner for more love or exiting the relationship and reaching for a new partner rather than the extra cheeseburger. I am also pointing out how fatally flawed our media messaging is. Photoshop is not typically used to turn an obese person into a skinny person or an ugly person into a pretty person; it's used to turn an already skinny person into a toothpick or an already pretty person into a flawless glamazon. Magazine covers circle cellulite on celebrities' outer thighs and blow it up into a larger picture; the most miniscule of "flaws" is, quite literally, put under a microscope. Our common fear of people finding our physical flaws and focusing on them is warranted because it happens often and to all of us. But even if someone finds yours, you must remember that the discovery of minor physical "imperfections" (see? I hate that word) is not synonymous with the discovery of the reason a relationship ended or never began.

Unattractiveness is not a fatal flaw to bring to a relationship. Addictions, be they to work, drugs, alcohol, exercise, or anything else, are fatal flaws to bring to a relationship. Violence and emotional cruelty are fatal flaws to bring to a relationship. Slightly crooked noses, stretch marks, and cellulite do not create distance in relationships. Before you hang your head in shame while walking away from the type of relationship in which your appearance was blamed for its demise, consider that you didn't actually want to be with that person for even one more day. If your partner was consistently unkind to you, you don't want to be with them anymore; it is a universal truth that nobody wants to be in constant pain. If your partner was physically and/or emotionally unavailable to you, whether she worked too much or he was drunk all the time or some other reason, you not only don't want to be with them anymore, you can't. This is because it is impossible to be with someone who is not present in a coherent state. If somebody dumps you, before blaming yourself and your appearance for your current loneliness, remind yourself how lonely you were in such a painful, distant relationship. Trust me; it is better to receive no messages than to receive messages full of unkind words from a boyfriend/girlfriend/wife/husband. Embrace the lack of negativity; embrace the clean slate.

I am a collection of my unique traits—the artwork I create, the jokes I make, the words on these very pages, the acts of kindness I commit, and my character. Our bodies and faces are just vessels that carry our unique, authentic selves, which we have to offer the world. I want to surround myself with people who value my authentic self more than the package it comes in, and I believe all of you do, too. If you haven't found them yet, keep looking until you do.

21 – THE BENEFIT OF THE DOUBT

Ancient drawings and paintings of Jesus, who is believed to be the son of God, all portray him as a young, fit (complete with six-pack abs), bearded, conventionally attractive, white man. A large percentage of the world's population has no problem believing he performed miracles and continues to do so, despite no one having any tangible evidence to prove it. He is, in effect, given the benefit of the doubt. People worship him, and I often wonder... if he was unattractive, would people still worship him? Our culture is narcissistically obsessed with appearance and tends to rank the physically attractive higher than the unattractive, so it's not a coincidence that

Jesus was depicted as an attractive person. If God was, in fact, female, would anyone believe in her?

The benefit of the doubt that is extended to Jesus is also extended to virtually everyone who looks like him, i.e., white men, in our American culture. White men do not have to prove themselves capable of anything to be thought amazing and good—the majority automatically assume they are. More opportunities and dollars are handed to unqualified men than to the overqualified women next to them. The presidency was even handed to an unqualified man in 2016. Men's worth is confirmed via word of mouth, without question—a friend said he's a good guy, so he's believed to be as such. It's the same with God—a lot of people say he's male, he's good, and he's real, so he is believed to be as such. No background check is performed, and no references are called. Word of mouth is enough for many people to believe in God. A white man's resume may be entirely fabricated, but people will believe he has skills, nonetheless. I believe Jesus' resume of turning water into wine and walking on water was entirely fabricated, but people have given him the benefit of the doubt for centuries. He still got to lead the masses—he got the job.

Donald Trump, a man with no political track record or proven leadership capabilities, has just been elected to lead the most powerful country in the world, the

USA. A lot of people who voted for him believe he can do the job well because he's a white man. He was given the benefit of the doubt. In our society, both at large and, particularly, in the corporate world, white men's ideas are given the benefit of the doubt. The ideas they put forth are automatically assumed to be good and acted upon immediately, whereas a female must PROVE her idea will work first and receive permission from a group before it is put into action. Take Obamacare, for example. Donald Trump stated that he wants to repeal Obamacare, and although he had no idea with what he would replace it, people voted for him. He literally had no plan, and people gave him the benefit of the doubt that he would come up with one. As of July 2017, he still hasn't successfully rolled out the new plan.

Throughout the 2016 U.S. presidential election, Hillary Clinton had to prove herself qualified for the job. A lifetime politician with decades of experience, she faced relentless doubts about her capabilities and the feasibility of her plans for the country. Meanwhile, Trump threw out lofty, infeasible ideas about building a wall along the southern border, a plan that would cost $25 billion that America obviously does not have to spare, but votes were given to move the plan forward. It was assumed to be a good idea because it came from a white man, who people believed capable of following through.

Personally, I found it sickening to watch Hillary Clinton lose the election. Our history of all male presidents does not hide the blatant sexism in America. A large portion of the population proved on November 8, 2016 that it is still not comfortable with a woman in power. SO uncomfortable, in fact, that they'd elect a person who hates more than half of the population to govern them. Donald Trump offended nearly everyone who isn't a heterosexual, Christian white man—women, homosexuals, Muslims, African Americans, Mexicans, etc.— and he STILL won. I'll admit that even I once gave him the benefit of the doubt, but of a different kind. I once doubted that he actually meant the things he said and thought he was trying to piss off as many people as he could in an effort to "throw" the election and make it easier for Hillary Clinton to win. Regardless of whether he was sincere or not, I was voting for Clinton. However, countless people who voted for him didn't believe the disparaging remarks he made about their "kind" and continued to vote for him. They still believed he was better suited for the job than a qualified woman.

My recurring thought on election night was, "If we (women) can't win the White House when the competition is a raging, misogynistic, sexual predator with zero political experience who seemingly hates everyone that isn't a rich white man, how are we ever going to win?"

Imagine the landslide that could have ensued if Clinton had actually been facing a qualified Republican competitor who was a decent person! The 2016 election should have been a slam dunk for her to win. If it were a basketball tournament, it would have been the #1 seed (Clinton) vs. the #16 seed (Trump). But it wasn't a basketball game. No one assumed she could score the points herself; they would have to be given to her. She must prove her ideas will work first and receive permission to move forward.

We can't continue like this. This culture of doubting women and making it hard, nay, impossible, for them to realize their dreams is costing every one of us in this country. By not backing the ideas women have, we are forcing them to dream smaller dreams and halting innovative progress. I've heard many a woman describe her dream and immediately follow her comments with, "But it'll never get funding," or "But it probably won't take off," and then she doesn't even try. We KNOW how hard it is to have our ideas heard in the first place, let alone put into action. Imagine the birthing and childcare advancements we could have today if women's ideas were automatically acted upon and allowed a chance to succeed before assuming they would fail. Nobody knows those two fields better than women, so plenty of them know how to improve either or both. A lot of us don't even pursue our dreams because we know that by the time we received funding and/or permission to do so, we'd be out of energy to do what we wanted to do in the first place. Lately, I, too, have been questioning whether it's worth chasing my dreams in America.

Hillary Clinton wanted to lead a lot of people who didn't want her to lead them. The entire four years would have been an uphill battle for her, so perhaps it's a blessing that she didn't win. In my opinion, the sane thing for Clinton to do would be to move to Scandinavia and try to run a country that's okay with either a male or female leader. It'd be easier on her mental and physical health, especially in her elder years, to run a country that will flow with her rather than tirelessly push back. My experiences at work have been that every idea I have faces a barrage of doubt and criticism; I dream of a world where women's ideas are not assumed to be bad until proven otherwise. I dream of a world where female ideas are given equal consideration as are male dreams. There's no reason why they shouldn't be. If the reason they aren't is because people believe Jesus was a man, so men are miraculous and women aren't—well, let's change that belief!

Imagine if the images of Jesus were of a black woman. Would we all be voting for Michelle Obama, funding her visions for this country without a flicker of doubt that they might not work? If Jesus were portrayed as an unattractive black woman, would women be free to look however they choose? Would men be proving themselves to women, asking us for jobs and raises and for our permission to move forward with their plans? It seems the sexism and racism in America started with religious beliefs that a white man was miraculous and all who look like him are superior to all others. We should be smarter than this. Just because someone looks like someone else does not mean they have the same capabilities. Looking like a president (typically older, white, and male) does not qualify one to be president, in the same way that looking like a doctor on TV does not qualify someone to save lives. So, what do we do to fix this status quo that oppresses women and entitles men? I don't think humans should change the image of God to be female, so that we can flip-flop our ranking. The inverse of a problem is not the solution. We also could not depict an all-inclusive god to remove all rankings. There are too many different skin colors, faces, body types, and sexes on this planet to do so. What we need to do is stop believing a white man died to save us all and start working together to save ourselves. And I mean all types people (black, white, male, female, elderly, children, etc.) should work together to save ALL types of people (not just white men).

Jesus hasn't shown up for years to prove he's real, and people are still reading the book he allegedly inspired and following the rules he allegedly set forth. Instead of believing that he is real and the most qualified to help you with a problem, you have the option to assume YOU and your fellow humans are the most qualified to help you. Instead of believing only a man can help you solve your problem or lead you, you have the option to believe a woman can help and lead. Maybe you need water for your crops, and you're thinking of praying to God for rain. You're not sure he's real because he doesn't ever appear or speak to you, but the people at the irrigation company in your state are definitely real and even answer the phone. Call them and believe in them. And when you get that irrigation system in place, thank the people who installed it—not God.

We also need to fight our instincts. Most of us have been programmed from a very young age to doubt and reject the ideas of females outright. When a female approaches you with an idea that may or may not work, give it a chance before you decide against it. You'll make her life easier by not draining her energy, and the idea she has may just make your life easier, too.

ESTABLISHING THE STATUS QUON'T

22 – EVOLVING WITH THE STATUS QUOS THAT HAVE ALREADY CHANGED

In 2017, women are still the oppressed gender, but they've come a long way. Women comprise more of the American workforce than men and are now more likely to earn college degrees than men. As women rise and grasp more power, establishing their independence, they need "others" less.

When people need each other, as opposed to simply wanting to be around each other, the tolerance for inappropriate behavior is higher. In the same way that a child will tolerate physical abuse from a parent because he relies on his parents for food, a woman may tolerate violence from her husband because she relies on him for money. Independent people realize that once they can meet their own needs, there is no reason to be around someone who treats them poorly; they're better off on their own or with people who treat them well. The rise in the divorce rate in recent years is concrete evidence of this phenomenon. Statistics show that wives file more divorces than husbands. As women need their husbands less, they're forced to evaluate whether they want them, and many of them have decided that they don't. The wheels of change are already in motion—the status quo of the wife relying financially on her husband has already been overturned. Many people are happy about this change and contributing to the momentum, while others still need to catch up.

As a woman who is gainfully employed, has health insurance, and owns her own condo, I don't need a man in order to survive. Therefore, in the dating world, I am trying to find a man I *want* to be around, not one I *need* to be around. In order to keep our romantic relationship going, he must provide something other than money and a home to live in—he must keep me interested. Plenty of other women are out there in the dating pool trying to achieve the same goal. Thanks to sperm banks, women no longer even need a man to have a child. I can sense the unease from the men in the dating world, for they are now in a position that women have been in all our lives—trying to attract and keep a mate interested who does not need us for survival. Women learned a long time ago how to make men want them, and it spawned the whole cosmetics industry. Plenty of the men I've met show how green they are in the game of attraction. It used to be enough to pay for all the meals and drive her around in a fancy car during the courtship phase, but now women are splitting the check and asking what else these men can bring to the table... kindness? compassion? empathy? We only want someone who can make our lives better, and material gifts are not the universal love language for women, so some men are struggling.

It is commonplace to talk about the gender pay gap these days, but hardly anyone mentions the gender emotional development gap. Women have been developing their emotional skills for hundreds of years. Our gender was kept out of the workforce for a long time, so we had to contribute in other ways to relationships and marriage: emotional support was the most common. As a result, it was socially acceptable more for a woman to display emotion, talk about feelings, and seek therapeutic support. Women supported their men emotionally but found their own support through their, often female, social networks while their men were at the office. Rather than building a network of fulfilling friendships, many men focused solely on work and their wives. Women had a head start.

Now that we have full access to the working world, women are finding that we desire our mates to have the same traits that we possess. We want emotional support from a man or no man at all. Our relationships with women provide emotional support, so we've come to expect it in all our relationships. We want a man who is an equal, rather than someone who completes us. A lot of us have spent our time developing the traits that we lacked, rather than looking to a man to provide them. It feels silly to be in a romantic relationship with someone who doesn't want to listen to you or spend time with you (due, perhaps, to long hours at the office) when you have a network of friends and family who do. Those non-romantic relationships then become what fulfill you and make you happy, which can prompt you to question whether you even need the romantic relationship. I have found it frustratingly difficult to find a male with a level of emotional development equal to my own, particularly because it's not socially acceptable and definitely not status quo for him to have that level of development. To bridge the gap in emotional intelligence between the sexes, each must first acknowledge that it exists.

Closing the emotional development gap will benefit both genders. Men will be able to release feelings and tears they may have otherwise suppressed, possibly already beginning to manifest as illnesses. Women will feel more supported having partners who are more in tune with their needs. Also, each gender will better understand the other because they will better understand themselves.

I hope the men who have focused exclusively on physical beauty in a woman are now seeing how difficult it is to always try to be desirable, so a mate will choose to be with you or stay with you. Perhaps if they understand what they've been putting women through, they'll ease up on expecting them to look pretty all the time. Men used to have their pick of the litter. If they didn't think their wife was pretty or obedient anymore, they could go out and impregnate a prettier, younger girl down the street. These days, that prettier girl probably already has a job and owns the house she lives in. She doesn't need this married man and will reject him to pursue one who is emotionally available.

I do think men can safely assume a complete role reversal is not about to take place, though. Women have already learned to value men for who they are, rather than how they look. We know how bad it feels to be constantly objectified and deemed worthy or worthless based on our physical appearance, so most of us have no desire to make someone else feel that way. We're not going to objectify men, but we're also not going to accept them objectifying us. Female friendships and social networks are on the rise, and we're supporting each other, making emotionally immature men even less desirable.

Social media has given everyone a voice, and each gender is still learning what has been expected of the other. As men begin to get in touch with their emotions and tears, women will hopefully accept their increased sensitivity. The genders cannot become equals without each supporting the other's conscious development of the traits that they lack. My hope is that the status quon't will be complete beings who seek out interdependent partners, rather than codependent people seeking fillers for the cracks in their hearts and psyches.

23 – FRAMILY

I have two living parents, a brother, and a sister. I entered this world knowing they would never leave me because they were supposed to stick around—it's what family does. I just didn't realize until many years later that I would ever want to leave some of them. One thing I've always known, though, is that no one besides family is expected to stay by your side no matter what happens. Friendships end and people understand because these relationships began by choice. Similarly, even though marriages begin with a promise to stay together forever, most people understand when one ends because that relationship began by choice. Society generally expects if you didn't choose to begin a relationship (i.e., with your blood relatives), then you should not choose to leave it.

The phrase "blood is thicker than water" is meant to imply the strength of a familial bond and has some truth in it. It is very hard to sever a familial bond, though I would argue that is because of societal pressures rather than shared bloodlines. And regardless of how hard it is to sever a bond, that doesn't mean it should never be done.

When the pain of being around certain family members became too difficult to bear, I moved away. I didn't fully close the door on long-distance relationships with them for a while, however, because I was afraid I wouldn't be able to find new people who I could trust to never leave me. When one relative became an alcoholic and certain family members leaned on me way too hard for emotional support, I snapped. The emotional influence of those long-distance relationships nearly drove me crazy, and they cost me several months of sleep. The family couldn't physically leave me because we already lived so far apart, and they never said the words that would end our relationships, but their actions did. A person who is drunk all the time is not in a relationship anymore, because they are not emotionally present. A person who expects you to catch every one of their teardrops is not in a relationship with you, because you're not allowed to lean back on them. Relationships are a two-way street, but several of mine had become entirely one-sided.

Our culture tends to point fingers at the person who says the words that end a relationship. The person who actually says, "I don't want to be with you anymore," is made out to be the "bad guy" and accused of abandonment. If a pathetic drug addict who has lost her job and been absent-minded for years gets dumped by her boyfriend or divorced by her husband, some people will say, "how could he leave her in her time of need? What about their vows to be there for better or for worse?" They don't realize that even though she has physically been there with him, she left him emotionally a long time ago, and he can't take it anymore. I am the bad guy in the relationships I have ended with certain family members. I said the words and moved on.

Deciding to pull away from those people was scary because I thought I had to replace each person I was letting go of, one for one. I thought staying away from extended family gatherings at the holidays would mean I'd have even MORE people to replace—aunts, uncles, cousins, etc. I also thought it would take a long time to get to know people I could trust to stick around, and I was afraid I could only find one or two. However, the relationships I ended had been so emotionally disconnected that trading two severed relationships for one really supportive friend was an even trade. Similar math can be done with acquaintances or distant relatives. For example, a relationship with one trustworthy, reliable friend can be more fulfilling than relationships with twelve acquaintances. I've also found in my personal experience that if I can be my authentic self immediately with a new friend, that relationship can be much more fulfilling than a lifelong relationship I've had with a distant relative. Time and blood do not determine how fulfilling a relationship will be.

The 2015 holiday season was the first one I spent away from my family during which I didn't feel guilty for not having gone home. I had known for years that I didn't enjoy my holidays when I spent them back home, so a few years ago, I stopped going. However, the guilt I felt for not going those first couple of years was almost as painful as the experience of going home had been. In order to convince myself it was okay to not go, I had to remind myself over and over how badly I had been hurt emotionally and would continue to be if I went home. I talked about the people who hurt me in therapy, a support group, with friends, and with a very supportive aunt for years. When I got tired of talking about them, I would see them in my dreams. The reminders from my subconscious as to what I have been through and now have moved past are ever present, encouraging me to care of myself and choose my company wisely.

I had other dreams that led me to understand what I truly want and don't want. A few dreams involved me being in a house or an apartment with all the doors and windows shut and people trying to get in through the windows. In the dream, I keep closing the windows, and when the people outside the house break the windows, I close the blinds. I learned from these dreams that I am inside a proverbial new house, and I want to keep old, painful ties to people who hurt me out of it. This is true in my real life. I bought a condo, and only loving people are welcome in my household.

Pulling away from my family left room for me to create a *framily*, or friends I consider family. I'm at ease with my framily because I can express how I truly feel to them. These people share in my joy when I need to celebrate, and they comfort me when I'm in pain. In general, they treat all my feelings as valid, and I treat theirs the same. I don't feel I have to impress them in order to be loved.

I met some of my framily members at support group meetings. I started attending these meetings around the holidays one year because I didn't want to go home but didn't have any other place to go. They welcomed me with open arms and would do so for you, too. Regardless of how many meetings you attend, you can make connections with people who will spend holidays with you and friends you can have, potentially, for life. Meetings exist that are tailored to people from a variety of backgrounds (alcoholics, family members of alcoholics, romance addicts, men who stuff their feelings, etc.). By being at the same meeting, you've already established common ground and have something to talk about. You've also both expressed a common goal to improve your lives, and your bond will deepen as you share that journey together.

24 – THE EARTH, THE EARTH, THE EARTH IS ON FIRE

A popular song by the Bloodhound Gang called "The Roof Is on Fire" was released in 1996. The chorus repeats "the roof, the roof, the roof is on fire" and ends with "we don't need no water let the motherf*cker burn, burn motherf*cker, burn." I wonder if this band had any idea their song about a roof would describe the exact attitude many people would take toward the earth several years later. Religious or not, plenty of folks are denying that climate change and global warming are occurring, despite all scientific and common-sense evidence to the contrary. In other words, "We don't need no water let mother earth burn."

When a person calls the fire department because his house is on fire, the firefighters show up and put it out with water. Mother Earth is doing the exact same thing; she's heating up, so much so that wildfires are happening in some areas, and she's melting her ice caps to put out the flames. Our once beautiful, blue and green earth has become scorched. Why is she on fire in the first place? Because of humans. Humans have created factories and cars that emit pollutants and gasses that collect in the atmosphere and trap heat on earth. These same gasses are thinning the ozone, which is earth's sunscreen. However, this is a sunscreen that we cannot simply reapply every thirty minutes. Once it's gone, we're exposed. The sun's rays are burning through the atmosphere from the outside, and we're burning through it from the inside. Our roof is, quite literally, on fire.

Some humans are more to blame than others for climate change, but that doesn't matter. Regardless of whether we created the problem, we can all help solve it. We can all recycle, use renewable energy, conserve water, and go paperless (deforestation is also contributing to global warming). However, we will not make a measurable impact and a sustainable difference unless we identify our common need for a habitable environment, rather than monetary compensation, as the only valid incentive to solve the problem. Currently, plenty of people are refusing to protect and/or clean the environment unless they'll be paid to do so.

Unfortunately, capitalism stands in the way of many of the environmental protection efforts currently underway. Rather than share the clean air that we have, people are selling it in cans and bags to the Chinese, who are living with air pollution so severe it's affecting their health. Rather than purify the drinking water pumped to our homes via modern plumbing, Dasani and Evian were created to charge money for pure water. Brown water, full of lead, was pumped into homes in Flint, Michigan to save money. Energy companies are offering their customers renewable energy sources, but for a higher premium. Fruit and vegetables, which grow on trees and in the ground, cost more than processed, packaged food made in factories that are polluting the environment. As time goes on, health and safety are becoming a luxury afforded to the rich, rather than a right granted to us all. It is a bleak reality that a person, company, city, or even country may or may not be able to monetarily afford to protect humans' health and the environment.

Environmental protection efforts are just as important as a societal character shift away from greed. One will not work without the other. In my opinion, rather than charging people extra for making environmentally safe and healthy choices, fines should be imposed on those who DON'T make them. Society needs to shift the cost to those who are putting all of our lives in danger. To do this, everyone must be involved. Energy companies would need to change their fee structures to make the environmentally safe choice the cheaper choice. Every person on earth would need to be conscious of his everyday decisions. Although individually we may not be able to fix the existing environmental problems, we each can make an impact by not creating new problems or worsening those we're currently dealing with.

Just like capitalism, many Christian people are thwarting environmental protection efforts. Plenty of these folks assume that God will take care of us and either clean up the Earth or move us to a new planet when Earth becomes an unsafe environment in which to live. Trusting that everything happening around us, including smog-filled skies and plastic-filled oceans, is "part of God's plan," they're not making an effort to change. They are praying for a divine solution to a human problem, which is strange, given their Bible talks about a time when God didn't protect humans from an environmental problem—a flood. The story can be found in the book of *Genesis*. *Genesis 6:5-8* reads:

"The LORD saw that the wickedness of man was great in the earth, and that every intention of the thoughts of his heart was only evil continually. And the LORD regretted that he had made man on earth, and it grieved him to his heart. So the LORD said, "I will blot out man whom I have

created from the face of the land, man and animals and creeping things and birds of the heavens, for I am sorry that I have made them. But Noah found favor in the eyes of the LORD."

How do you feel after reading that? Do you feel safe? Does it not read, "I wish most of you had never been born"? It's the exact same thing as parents saying their pregnancy was a mistake. If you believe the Bible is full of nothing but inarguable truth, then this particular pill must be extremely painful to swallow. I don't understand how anyone whose religion is based on the Bible could believe their god could be trusted to fix the environment and save the humans that live in it. In this particular story, he chose his one favorite family and saved them — that's it! How would anyone know if he's going to pick them and their family to survive the next flood?

The story of Noah, who is said to be 600 years old in *Genesis 7:6*, is truly outrageous and goes on to document an alleged conversation between him and God. In this conversation, God tells Noah to build an ark (big wooden ship) for himself, his wife, and his sons and their wives to survive an impending forty-day rainstorm. Noah is instructed to bring two of every species of animal onto the ship (one male and one female) in order to release them after the flood to let them procreate. The story goes on to say the rains ceased after forty days but the flooding lasted for 150 days, at which point Noah, his family, and the animals allegedly came off the ship. It's unbelievable that a group of people could bring enough food on board for all humans and animals to survive for 150 days. We all know that most animals eat other animals, and yet Christians are supposed to believe the circle of life paused while everyone was on that ship.

Think of the infamous "poop cruise" in 2013. A Carnival cruise ship's engine caught fire, stranding people in a ship with no power, overflowing toilets, rationed food, total darkness and little drinking water for days in the Gulf of Mexico. That ship had toilets on it, but plumbing was not invented when the ark would have been constructed by this alleged 600-year-old man. Given fruits and vegetables are inedible within days of being picked, and there would be nowhere to grow them on board a ship, Noah and his family could not have survived 150 days in a dark wooden ship without eating at least some of the animals on board. They also could easily have spread disease from their own onboard excrement and died. I can say, with absolute certainty, that this story was entirely made up and never happened. Given the story of Noah and the flood, it would not only be ineffective to pray to the Christian god to save us from global warming, it'd be unwise. Based on his track record, he'd be more likely to wipe us out than to help us!

I learned the story of Noah and the ark as a kid, but it was cast in a positive light. Rather than focus on the verses immediately prior to those in which God rejects everyone but this chosen family and wants to kill all mankind, we were taught the verses about building an ark. I can even remember a coloring book with a picture of an ark and animals walking into it two by two. My little mind was manipulated to marvel at how God wanted to save the animals and protect Noah and to completely gloss over what he allegedly did to all the other people on earth. In fact, all I remembered was that coloring book, something about pairs of animals, and forty days of unknown significance until I googled the verses to write this chapter. I'm as shocked at what I read as you may be right now.

As with all the other points I've made in this book, your belief in God or lack thereof does not matter as long as it doesn't completely guide your life and prevent you from helping other people. You could believe in the Christian god and that the story of Noah and the Ark actually happened and still conclude that God isn't going to fix our earthly environment. Alternatively, you could believe God isn't real and still conclude that it's up to humans to save the environment. The status quon't is one of free thought and human collaboration, and I hope we see that in my lifetime.

Since God isn't going to save us from the earth catching on fire and flooding, we have to work together to save ourselves. Unfortunately, we are saving ourselves from ourselves, because we're the ones heating Mother Earth up to the point where she feels like she needs a flood to put out the flames. It's tough to admit that we are both the problem and the solution, but if all mankind can acknowledge this via self-reflection, they will care enough to act. People are more likely to act when the outcome will affect them personally, even if they won't be monetarily compensated. Admittedly, a lot of us probably wouldn't stage protests until we were dealing with a smog problem like the one present in China or a lead water problem like the one present in Flint, Michigan right now. But, if we wait until the problems in China and Flint plague the rest of the earth, it'll be too late. We won't have anywhere left to go to breathe clean air and drink clean water. Prevention is just as important as resolution, when it comes to the environment. Some people use religion as their reason to care about things and work toward solutions, but as you can see from this chapter, plenty of others use it as their reason not to. I hope this chapter has shed light on the fact that the divine safety net isn't there. We can't all move to Mars if the earth goes up in flames or drowns in a flood.

We're all in danger, and if you're not helping solve the problem, you are making it worse. Praying is the same as inaction when it comes to the environment, so get off your knees and recycle, write to your representatives, and go paperless. Start there.

25 – YOUR PERSONAL CONTRIBUTION

In many ways, the world around us is falling apart. The polar ice caps are melting, the climate is changing, terrorist groups are wreaking havoc on otherwise safe communities, and so on. All of these things are scary, but maybe they have to happen, so that humanity will fall together.

Religious leaders have spoken out against some of their time-honored traditions recently. Pope Francis is the first Catholic leader to have publicly stated that a person does not need to believe in God and follow Catholicism to get into heaven. Similarly, the Dalai Lama encouraged people to work for peace, rather than pray for peace, after the terrorist attacks in November

2015. He acknowledged that humans created the problem and that it would be up to humans to solve it.

While the terrorist attacks were not carried out by the Pope's or Dalai Lama's followers, perhaps the attacks spoke volumes to these two men about religion, in general. I think the Pope and the Dalai Lama may have wondered why the gods they believe in didn't intervene and stop the attacks. I know I did. Regardless of the thoughts and feelings these two religious/spiritual leaders had, I hope they saw the attacks as evidence of what can happen when people feel a stronger need to be right than to coexist and even survive. A belief itself does not divide people, but, rather, the idea that it needs to be shared by all people.

We cannot control what other adults believe, no matter how hard we may try. Despite our different beliefs, our humanity unites us. Catholic or Jewish, religious or not, we all take a minute to reflect on our own lives and gain perspective when a tragedy happens. We all understand the tragedy could just as easily have been our own, had we been in that place at that time. We realize we have been given another day on this earth, while others have not. Millennials remember where they were when the planes crashed into the twin towers in New York City on September 11. Baby Boomers remember where they were when they learned President

Kennedy had been assassinated. Witnessing something terrible makes you immediately thankful for what you have; it's simply human nature. Without tragedy, there is no widespread call to help each other—to put our differences aside and come together. We have that call now, and my hope is that people will stop trying to get everyone on the same page and simply embrace the different chapters in the book of humanity.

As I was preparing to write this book, I researched similar books that had already been published. As a child who was spiritually abused, I searched for books of that nature, but what I noticed was that each book ended with a chapter or two on how the author had landed back in the Christian faith and church. My book does not end this way. In the true spirit of challenging the status quo, I don't recommend anyone go back to what broke them just because it's what everyone has been doing. What broke me was the Christian church, my parents, and my grandparents.

You really needn't identify with a particular religion, political party, football team, fandom, support group, etc. Who you are will inevitably evolve with your experiences, anyway. I used to be a total party girl, identifying with a particular crowd that liked to stay out late. Now, I identify as a bit of a homebody, only the group, by nature, does not get together! What I mean is, don't worry about being like everyone else or even being like yourself. You may not know who you really are yet, so trying to be like you once were could be the less fulfilling move for you. Likewise, don't worry about being someone no one has ever been before. Just because a path has been paved, that does not mean it's the easier one to take.

Consider wearing tennis shoes and walking along a sidewalk next to a well-manicured front lawn. It is no more difficult to walk along the sidewalk than it is to walk in the grass. You will reach the same destination if you walk across the grass as you will if you walk along the sidewalk, and walking through the grass may even get you there quicker. Someone building a sidewalk and wanting you to use it does not mean you must or that it will make your life easier if you do. Similarly, someone handing you a Bible and wanting you to use it as a guide for life does not mean it will make your life better. From personal experience, I can tell you that using the Bible to guide your life can actually make your life a whole lot harder. For me, it was a shaming, emotionally painful way to live.

Maybe you're thinking, "I don't follow the teachings of the Bible because I think they'll make my life easier; I follow them because I'm afraid of the wrath of God." If that is the case, I ask you to remember that your belief in God was not your own. Left to our own devices, we would not all dream up the same stories of Adam and Eve, Jesus on the cross, etc. You can change your beliefs like you can change your hair color. When you are a child, you do have fewer choices than you do when you are an adult. In order for your parents to feed, clothe, and shelter you, you have to do a lot of things they tell you to do. This may include going to church, praying certain prayers, pretending to like certain people, pretending to hate certain people, and so on. If you later renounce the things you did as a kid, it is important to have compassion for the position you were in. Try not to judge yourself for going along with something that now repulses you. Maybe you had to do it so you would get your next meal. Similarly, you need to realize you are no longer in those circumstances. You have a choice to never do whatever that thing is again, because you are now an adult. Having been conditioned to make a particular choice or do a certain thing will also no longer excuse you from the responsibility for continuing to make that choice, because you are no longer dependent on your parents. If the only reason you are doing something is, "because that's what I've always done," that is not a valid reason.

I highly recommend reading self-help books. They can make you feel less alone until you find people with whom to discuss them. If you haven't met someone who lives near you that would understand what you've been through and why you feel the way you do, sometimes you can find that person in a book. I found solace in Alice Miller's books. I never got the chance to meet her, but for a while it was enough for me to know that someone, at some point in time, had felt the same way I did. Alice made radical choices. She wrote the truth about her parents, and she encouraged her readers to speak their truths, as well. I had wanted to separate from some biological family members for a while, but I hadn't been consciously aware of that fact until I read her books. Alice's story was one of physical and sexual abuse, so her advice was for readers in similar situations. While I experienced a different type of abuse, I came to the same conclusion. I also felt compelled to write my own book, in hopes that readers who have experienced religious abuse, like me, will feel less alone. Even if you don't make any changes in your life, I hope you find at least a small measure of peace in knowing that I've felt the same way you do now. You are not the only one. And if you can't find a book that speaks to your story, then write your own book!

In some support groups and most religions, people learn that they are not in control of all their circumstances and that they can pray to a higher power for help with anything beyond their reach. Some people take this lesson too far, however, and instead of folding their hands in prayer, they sit on them. They completely avoid taking action in their own life and leave everything up to their higher power.

You have many more options in your lives than you may realize. It's status quo to blame everyone else for our problems. I was guilty of this for years, and I'm making a conscious effort not to do it anymore. Plenty of people have similar backgrounds to my own, and we are in very different places in our lives. We are in those different places because we have made different choices. I chose to go to therapy for six years, read numerous self-help books, get an education, find a job, move away from the chaos of my family, find a support group, and establish a loving network of friends. Others have chosen to develop their own drinking problems, expect the world to feel sorry for them, and never move forward. The latter lifestyle is typically not recognized as a sum of active choices, but it is, nonetheless.

Loads of people want to complain endlessly about how lousy their partner is, but few people will cop to the fact that they chose to be with that person and are still choosing to stay with them. Plenty of people had parents who hit them when they were children and, in turn, hit their own children, claiming they don't know any better. It's no longer a viable excuse. There is too much information at our fingertips, and there are too many free support groups out there for anyone to have an excuse not to seek the help they need. Nobody who is an adult is a victim of circumstances anymore. We can all pray to God to solve our problems, or we can realize that God is within us and we are capable of working toward our own solutions. God is not going to drive us to a support group meeting or dial a number on our phone to inquire about a job. We have to use our own hands. I'm a firm believer in the concept of co-creation. I believe that we were put here by some sort of inexplicable universal force, but that our lives are the product of our choices and the universe's responses. If we make healthy, loving choices, the universe responds in kind, but if we do nothing, the universe does nothing.

Don't wait for God to show up. Show up for yourself. Don't wait for his love to come. Give your love to yourself. You've always had an endless supply of love to give, and religion can make you afraid to give it to the wrong person, including yourself. That love you have to give is meant for you, and I hope that once you begin to love yourself, you quon't stop. Don't continue the traditions that have been passed on to you, simply because they are traditions. Find a reason for doing what you do, and create your own traditions. Joy is enough of a reason to do something. Don't limit yourself to the existing state of affairs. Your presence here on earth will change it, regardless of what you do and no matter your choices. I just hope you recognize your unique thoughts and share them in a way that helps us evolve as a human race. Your personal contribution to humankind is your authentic self, so give us that.

ABOUT THE AUTHOR

Katilyn Pulcher grew up in a Baptist family in Missouri and became agnostic in her mid-twenties when a close relative became an alcoholic. Despite the enormous suffering the alcoholism caused her whole family, no amount of prayer improved that relative's situation. So, Katilyn decided that the Christian God must either not be listening to those prayers or not exist. In her late-twenties, Katilyn then struggled to heal her cumulative emotional pain by working a twelve-step program for family members of alcoholics, without a belief in a higher power. Upon entering the program, she discovered the bulk of her emotional pain stemmed, not from her exposure to alcoholism, but from the religious abuse she had endured during childhood. The constant verbal onslaught of criticism, perfectionism, and shame that came with religious fanaticism had completely shattered her self-worth. However, she was unaware of that fact until she began the twelve-step program.

Katilyn was unable to find true peace in working a twelve-step program, largely because the programs available to her demanded belief in a higher power and forgiveness of all the abuse she had endured—neither of which comes naturally to a survivor of religious abuse and both of which she discusses, at length, in this book. Rather than accepting the status quo—Christianity or twelve-step programs—as garden variety paths to inner peace, Katilyn thought for herself and wrote the status quon't.

Katilyn was unaware of support groups specific to survivors of religious abuse when she needed help and, thus, is actually grateful a relative became alcoholic so she could find help in the support groups tailored to family members of alcoholics. One of her dreams is for her story to reach other survivors of religious abuse who may or may not have been exposed to alcoholism, do not want to return to church, and, thus, do not know where to turn for support. In true status quon't fashion, however, she does not lay out a path toward inner peace—she will encourage you to find your own.

Made in the USA
Monee, IL
27 January 2024

52466022R00142